LAS VEGAS
ENCOUNTER

SARA BENSON

Las Vegas Encounter

Published by Lonely Planet Publications Pty Ltd
ABN 36 005 607 983

Australia	Head Office, Locked Bag 1, Footscray, Vic 3011 ☎ 03 8379 8000 fax 03 8379 8111 talk2us@lonelyplanet.com.au
USA	150 Linden St, Oakland, CA 94607 ☎ 510 250 6400 toll free 800 275 8555 fax 510 893 8572 info@lonelyplanet.com
UK	2nd fl, 186 City Rd London EC1V 2NT ☎ 020 7106 2100 fax 020 7106 2101 go@lonelyplanet.co.uk

This title was commissioned in Lonely Planet's Oakland office and produced by: **Commissioning Editor** Suki Gear **Coordinating Editor** Nigel Chin **Cartographer** Brendan Streager **Coordinating Layout Designer** Nicholas Colicchia **Assisting Editors** Barbara Delissen, Stephanie Pearson **Managing Editor** Liz Heynes **Managing Cartographer** Alison Lyall **Managing Layout Designer** Celia Wood **Cover Researcher** Naomi Parker, lonelyplanetimages.com **Internal Image Researcher** Sabrina Dalbesio, lonelyplanetimages.com **Thanks to** Yvonne Bischofberger, Glenn Garland, Mark Griffiths, Brigita Honkala, Lisa Knights

ISBN 978 1 74179 708 4

Printed by Hang Tai Printing Company, Hong Kong
Printed in China

HOW TO USE THIS BOOK

Color-Coding & Maps

Color-coding is used for symbols on maps and in the text that they relate to (eg all eating venues on the maps and in the text are given a green knife and fork symbol).

All items are mapped on the pull-out map.

Send us your feedback We love to hear from readers – your comments help make our books better. We read every word you send us, and we always guarantee that your feedback goes straight to the appropriate authors. The most useful submissions are rewarded with a free book. To send us your updates and find out about Lonely Planet events, newsletters and travel news visit our award-winning website: *lonelyplanet.com/contact*.

Note: We may edit, reproduce and incorporate your comments in Lonely Planet products such as guidebooks, websites and digital products, so let us know if you don't want your comments reproduced or your name acknowledged. For a copy of our privacy policy visit *lonelyplanet.com/privacy*.

SARA BENSON

First awestruck by the neon lights of the Strip during a cross-country trek from Chicago to California, Sara had a serendipitous one-night stand with Sin City that soon became a torrid love affair. Now she travels down to the desert every chance she gets, and has racked up more hours gambling, carousing and wandering around Las Vegas than she'll ever admit to her grandmother. She and her entourage have spent many a lost weekend nightclub-hopping down the Strip, feasting at star chefs' tables and playing poker until the wee hours in downtown's Glitter Gulch. Sara is also an avid outdoor enthusiast. Her articles have featured on popular travel websites and in magazines and newspapers from coast to coast, including the *Las Vegas Review-Journal*, *Los Angeles Times* and *National Geographic Traveler*. Keep up with Sara's latest adventures on her blog, the Indie Traveler (http://indietraveler.blogspot.com), or Twitter (@indie_traveler).

SARA'S THANKS

Many thanks to all of the Las Vegas residents, bloggers and tweeters who helped my research, especially those who took time out to be interviewed and photographed for this book. Without Mike Connolly, Suki Gear and Jennye Garibaldi, creating this book just wouldn't have been so much fun.

THE PHOTOGRAPHER

Jerry Alexander makes his home in the Napa Valley, California. He and his wife, Thanaphon, have just completed building a home in Chiang Mai, Thailand. Jerry grows grapes in the Napa Valley and after harvest he and his wife head back to Thailand to see family and friends – and capture images around Southeast Asia. Jerry has worked on six individual titles for Lonely Planet and contributed to many of Lonely Planet's guidebooks as well.

Cover photograph Cowgirl neon sign, Las Vegas, Lee Foster/LPI. **Internal photographs** p3, p41, p75, p124, p141 Sara Benson; p40, p164 Citycenter Land, LLC; p18 LOOK Die Bildagentur der Fotografen GmbH/Alamy; p86 Nick Hanna/Alamy; p106 Kelly-Mooney Photography/Corbis; p63 Paul Vidler/Alamy; p22 Rouse Photography. All other photographs by Lonely Planet Images and Jerry Alexander except p8, p93 Richard Cummins; p42, p177 John Elk III; p6 Lee Foster; p20 Jeff Greenberg; p14, p55, p60, p74, p96, p151, p155, p159, p172 Ray Laskowitz; p10 James Marshall; p19 Curtis Martin; p162 Carol Polich; p156 David Tomlinson

All images are copyright of the photographers unless otherwise indicated. Many of the images in this guide are available for licensing from **Lonely Planet Images**: www.lonelyplanetimages.com.

Enjoy a slice of the Big Apple at New York–New York (p53)

CONTENTS

Why is our travel information the best in the world? It's simple: our authors are passionate, dedicated travelers. They don't take freebies in exchange for positive coverage so you can be sure the advice you're given is impartial. They travel widely to all the popular spots, and off the beaten track. They don't research using just the internet or phone. They discover new places not included in any other guidebook. They personally visit thousands of hotels, restaurants, palaces, trails, galleries, temples and more. They speak with dozens of locals every day to make sure you get the kind of insider knowledge only a local could tell you. They take pride in getting all the details right, and in telling it how it is. Think you can do it? Find out how at **lonelyplanet.com**.

THIS IS LAS VEGAS

A Bible-toting Elvis kisses a giddy couple who've just pledged eternity in the Chapel of Love. A blue-haired granny feeds nickels into a slot machine while chain-smoking and slugging gin-and-tonics. A porn star saunters by a nightclub's velvet rope. Blink, and you'll miss it. Sleep? Fuhgeddaboutit.

Vegas is the ultimate escape. A few frenzied sleepless nights here can be more intoxicating than a week-long bender elsewhere. Let the everyday rules of behavior slide a little, like a burlesque dancer's feather boa. Be as naughty as you wanna be, and make your most devilish fantasies come true. Sin City stands ready to give you an alibi: what happens here, stays here. Who can resist such seductive temptation?

The defining mood of Las Vegas is euphoria, from the 19th-century silver miners looking to strike the mother lode to the mobsters, movie stars, showgirls and crooners who lived it up here during the 'fabulous' 1950s heyday. Eccentric billionaire Howard Hughes helped the city clean up its act when he ushered in corporate ownership of casinos, and soon afterward middle America invaded the hoity-toity Strip in their polyester tracksuits with screaming rug rats in tow. As the 20th century raced toward its end, megaresorts on par with Macau and Monte Carlo began to spike the Strip's skyline. Every decade has made Las Vegas more of a boomtown than ever before.

This city demands a suspension of disbelief, so don't take it too seriously. In Sin City, fate is decided by the spin of a roulette wheel. It's a place where lucky schmucks are treated like royalty and the rich wager thousands on a single roll of the dice. But in the end, it doesn't matter if you play the penny slots or lay down a bankroll at the poker tables; it's a sure thing you'll still leave town believing you've just had the most frenzied, fast-paced and fantastical time of your life.

Top left Put all your cards on the table at Caesars Palace (p43) **Bottom left** Savor the spectacle of Las Vegas

LAS VEGAS LAYOUT

Sprawled immodestly along Las Vegas Blvd, the Strip is constantly re-inventing itself, becoming ever more spectacular – and more of a spec-tacle. Every casino hotel has its own attractions, with plenty of action besides gaming. The Strip runs south to Mandalay Bay and north to the Stratosphere. Its nerve center is the intersection with Flamingo Rd.

Downtown presides over the distant north end of the tourist corridor, with the canopied Fremont Street Experience streaking down the middle of Glitter Gulch. The city's historic quarter is preferred by serious gamblers, who find faux volcanoes beneath them; the smoky, low-ceilinged casinos have changed little over the years. East of Las Vegas Blvd, Fremont St is undergoing a renaissance of cool, with independent bars and nightclubs popping up.

The 18b Arts District, emerging around the intersection of Main St and Charleston Blvd, is ground zero for hipsters, artists and alt-cultural types. The desolate stretch of Las Vegas Blvd between downtown and the Strip is nicknamed the Naked City. These downtrodden blocks sport tattered cheap motels, tattoo parlors and drive-thru wedding chapels.

East of the Strip, the University of Nevada (UNLV) campus attracts youthful carpetbaggers along Maryland Parkway. Anchored by the Las Vegas Convention Center, Paradise Rd streams south past the Hard Rock casino hotel into the Fruit Loop, the epicenter of the LGBT community.

West of the Strip, the Palms and Rio casino hotels rule the roost; many of Sin City's strip clubs and sex shops are hidden in industrial backstreets and strip malls. Burgeoning suburbs include Henderson, southeast of McCarran International Airport, and moneyed Summerlin, northwest near Red Rock Canyon.

Disorientation is a constant risk, whether you're searching for your hotel room, stumbling drunkenly through a casino, or desperately trying to remember where you parked the car.

Left Las Vegas welcomes all those visiting, whether for a little business or a whole lot of pleasure

>HIGHLIGHTS

Lap up the sun poolside at the Treasure Island Hotel & Casino (p61)

>1 STRIP SHOWS

DIVE INTO THE FREE-FOR-ALL ON THE STRIP

The sensory overload of blindingly bright neon lights signifies that yes, you've finally arrived on Las Vegas Blvd (aka the Strip). The infamous Strip has the lion's share of hulking casino hotels and mega-resorts, all flashily competing to lure you (and your wallet) inside. But good news for low rollers: some of the Strip's best stuff is free.

From the beacon shooting toward the stars out of the jet-black pyramid of the Luxor (p49) to the gaudily striped big top of Circus Circus (p44) to the gigantic Stratosphere Tower (p23), all of the Strip is a spectacle.

No first-time visitor should miss the dancing musical fountains of Bellagio (p80; pictured right), working the illusory magic that a small lake actually exists in the middle of the Mojave Desert.

Just up the street is the Mirage's exploding volcano (p81), recently remodeled to be even bigger and better than it was before.

Meanwhile, next door at TI (Treasure Island), the scantily clad Sirens of TI (p81) face off against hunky beefcake sailors in a hilariously bad, rock 'n' roll battle of the sexes that looks a lot like a Christina Aguilera video.

But that's not all. The opposite side of the Strip holds just as many distractions for freeloaders. Lean over the graceful bridges and balustrades of the Venetian (p62) and watch the singing gondoliers oar their boats through the mock canals of this Italianate casino.

CRUISING THE STRIP

If you're a Vegas first-timer and you're driving, make sure you do a few things. First, arrive after dark. Next, pull over and admire everything from afar. Finally, exit off the interstate and cruise the length of Las Vegas Blvd (aka the Strip). Your eyes will pop out of your head, we bet.

Warning: don't attempt driving the Strip after 9pm on Friday or Saturday night, when weekend traffic will be gridlocked. No wheels? No problem! Ride the Ace or double-decker Deuce buses (p190), which run 24/7 along Las Vegas Blvd. Gray Line (p193) offers a night-time bus tour that lets you gawk at the city's neon lights.

Then hoof it down to Harrah's (p66), where the open-air Carnaval Court (p134) is a free, spring-break party every night, and the 'flair' bartenders juggle fire.

A short walk south is the kitschy Imperial Palace (p66), where 'dealertainers' (p78), dressed like celebrity impersonators (think Elvis, Tina Turner and Billy Idol), put on free song-and-dance shows on the casino floor.

>2 ARTS DISTRICT

PARTY WITH THE LOCALS ON FIRST FRIDAY NIGHTS

On the tattered fringes of downtown, hidden among the antiques shops and vintage-clothing stores (p88), is the city's emerging 18b Arts District. Drive by it on any given weekday and you might not even notice pivotal landmarks like the Arts Factory (p74; pictured above). But on the first Friday night of each month, these rundown streets take on a carnival atmosphere as 10,000 art lovers, hipsters, indie musicians and hangers-on turn it into one giant block party. Gallery openings, performance art, live music, fortune tellers and tattoo artists are all part of the fun at this fave event of locals. Show up and you might be the only tourist there – a nice change after buzzing around the crowded casinos and megaresorts on the Strip. For celebratory after-party drinks, head to the Beauty Bar (p134).

For more on the local arts scene, see p170.

>3 ATOMIC TESTING MUSEUM

EXAMINE THE LEGACY OF THE COLD WAR IN THE DESERT

During the atomic heyday of the 1950s, gamblers and tourists downtown stared mesmerized as mushroom clouds rose on the desert horizon, and the city crowned a Miss Atomic Bomb. Over the next four decades, over 900 nuclear explosions were initiated at the Nevada Test Site, just 65 miles northwest of the city.

Curious to know more? Buy your tickets at the replica of a Nevada Test Site guard station, then spend an hour or two browsing this awesome 8000-sq-ft Smithsonian-affiliated museum (p74). Multi-media exhibits focus on science, technology and the social history of the 'Atomic Age' (p180), which lasted from WWII until atmospheric bomb testing was driven underground in 1961 and a worldwide ban on nuclear testing was declared in 1992. 'Stewards of the Land' galleries examine Southern Nevada's past, present and future, from Native American ways of life to the environmental legacy of atomic testing, including the controversial Yucca Mountain nuclear-waste storage project.

Check out the temporary exhibits of contemporary art and real-life science near the front entrance. Next to them is the cool scientific and retro-minded museum shop, where you can buy your very own A-bomb fallout shelter sign or biohazard T-shirt.

HIGHLIGHTS

>4 CASINO MEMORABILIA

SHOP FOR ONE-OF-A-KIND GAMBLING SOUVENIRS

As if Las Vegas was ashamed of its own sordid but fascinating history (p179), old-school casinos are being demolished with the speed of a freight train to make room for ever bigger and swankier megaresorts on the Strip. The heyday of outrageous theme hotels is over, too, as one after another, Strip casino hotels trade their gaudy Egyptian gods and faux European landmarks for more chic, but ultimately boring, high-class luxury.

Nothing sticks around for very long in this town. But fans of Old Vegas can still pick up pieces of mobster- and Rat Pack–era casino hotels at fun, funky downtown shops like Retro Vegas (p98) or Gold & Silver Pawn (p99), where you might find vintage casino souvenirs, from Binion's Horseshoe ashtrays to Rat Pack–era gaming chips. Or take home your very own antique slot machine or roulette wheel from the Gamblers General Store (p99; pictured above).

Be sure to pay a visit to the 1940s and '50s casino hotels still standing on the Strip, such as the Sahara (p59) and the Tropicana (p69), to snap up logo souvenirs from the gift shop and filch cocktail swizzle sticks and free match books from the bar before these places also go the way of the imploded Stardust and New Frontier.

For more tips on finding vintage Las Vegas, see p176.

>5 CIRQUE DU SOLEIL

JOIN THE AUDIENCE OF AN AVANT-GARDE CIRCUS

During the heyday of the 'Fabulous Fifties,' the Dunes caused a delectable scandal by inviting bare-breasted showgirls to star in its show *Minsky Goes to Paris*; the Stardust imported real French showgirls the next year to star in its topless revue *Lido de Paris*. Both of those legendary casino hotels have since been demolished, and although topless revues still sell out on the Strip – think Bally's *Jubilee!* (p145) and the MGM Grand's *Crazy Horse Paris* (p145) – today it's Cirque du Soleil shows that rule the roost.

This fantastical Québec-born circus troupe seems tailor-made for Las Vegas, where spectacle is craved above all else. Whimsical costumes, high-flying aerial acrobatics and giant taiko drums add up to an electrifying atmosphere. Anyone can get caught up in the heart-pounding, sometimes scintillating, yet ultimately silly shows. Watch the bizarre clown antics of *Mystère* (p146; pictured above), the Strip's longest-running Cirque spectacular (since 1993); the aquatic sensation *O* at Bellagio (p42); the martial-arts-inspired moves of *Kà* (p145); the musical journey of *LOVE* (p146), a Fab Four tribute; or *Viva Elvis* (p147).

If you can't score tickets to a Cirque show (they're almost always sold out in advance), drop by Cirque's Revolution Lounge (p153) to get a taste of the fun-for-all carnival atmosphere.

>6 FIRESIDE LOUNGE
REFUEL LATE-NIGHT AT A RETRO STRIPSIDE HIDEAWAY

Booze, bodacious bodies and booty are what many come to Vegas for, in which case a drunken crawl along the Strip is just what the witch doctor ordered.

The launching pad of choice for a wild Vegas night is an ultra lounge (p152), where cocktails are mixed tableside by models, eye-popping go-go dancers shimmy or sky-high views (see the boxed text, p134) are the specialty of the house. But these are mere stepping stones to Vegas' nightclubs (p140), which are pure fantasyland environments where sin is back in style.

But when it's 4am and your feet hurt after shakin' your booty all night long, where are you gonna go? Escape all of the other tourists at the Peppermill casino's 24-hour Fireside Lounge (p134). Hidden on the North Strip, this pint-sized coffee shop, with its candy-bright neon lights and faux flickering fireplaces, is a beacon.

Take your lover by the hand and step inside, where the swingin' 1970s never ended. Here cooing couples nestle into low-lying couches to make out as they sip exotically colored tropical drinks. The psychedelic decor and special-effects water fountains will be almost as distracting as your cocktail waitress's slinky dress.

Before you know it, the sun will be breaking over Las Vegas Blvd: the perfect end to a wild night.

>7 FREMONT STREET

LET IT ALL HANG OUT IN DOWNTOWN'S HISTORIC GLITTER GULCH

When you've tired of the glitz of the Strip, ride the Ace or Deuce bus (p190) downtown to Fremont St. There you'll discover the city's original hurly-burly casino row, nicknamed Glitter Gulch. This old-school gambling ghetto sprang up beside the railroad tracks back in 1905, more than 40 years before Bugsy cruised down the highway from LA to build the Strip.

Although downtown gambling halls aren't glamorous like Vegas' megaresorts, their proximity to one another is a real plus. Even if you're drunk out of your gourd, you can easily stumble between half a dozen gaming joints here. Play the penny slots, munch a bunch of deep-fried Oreos and Twinkies, grab a 99¢ electric-blue-colored margarita in a 3ft-high plastic glass and buy a tacky T-shirt from a 'Sin City' souvenir shop, while the Fremont Street Experience's cheesy laser-light show (p80) flashes overhead.

The Strip can keep its high-limit poker rooms, VIP velvet ropes and million-dollar shopping arcades – here, everyone can afford to live like the King.

>8 LIBERACE MUSEUM

MAKE A PILGRIMAGE TO A SHRINE OF KITSCH

Known throughout the world as 'Mr Showmanship,' Liberace was awarded six gold records and garnered two stars on the Hollywood Walk of Fame. Following his death in 1987, just a few months after his final public performance at New York's Radio City Music Hall, the late great entertainer was honored by the creation of this outrageous museum (p79).

While audiences enjoyed listening to Liberace's exuberant keyboard artistry, they were also amazed and secretly amused by his outlandish style: priceless pianos, like a rhinestone-encrusted Baldwin and a concert grand covered in mirrors; glittering Rolls-Royces and other exotic cars used to make stage entrances and exits; and fabulous million-dollar furs, feathered capes and sequined suits that are as frighteningly odd as they are funny.

You'll enjoy it all more if you time your visit to coincide with one of the free guided tours led by mad 'Red Hatter' fans, during which no mention will be made of Liberace's homosexuality, his death of AIDS-related complications or the more creepily bizarre rumors that he had his lover (who also happened to be his bodyguard and chauffeur) undergo plastic surgery in order to make him look more like Liberace himself.

>9 MANDALAY BAY BEACH

LAZE BY THE POOL ALL DAY

Las Vegas thrives on a pop culture of excess. Ever since Steve Wynn launched the fabulous Polynesian-themed Mirage casino hotel at the end of the no-holds-barred, money-rules-everything 1980s, every megaresort has aimed to be the biggest and best.

That also applies to resort swimming pools. Despite daunting competition from other casino hotels – such as Hard Rock (p48), with its Tahitian-style cabanas and swim-up blackjack, and downtown's Golden Nugget (p47), which has a water slide that shoots swimmers through a glass-enclosed shark tank – the city's most impressive guests-only pool complex is at Mandalay Bay (p50).

'M-Bay' imported 2700 tons of Southern Californian sand to build its artificial beach, where board-riders surf on 6ft-high artificial waves. Grab an inner tube and float away on a 'lazy river' ride, or rent a beachfront cabana or private villa and be royalty for a day. There's an air-conditioned beachside casino, where you can while away the hottest part of the day playing blackjack, roulette and craps. Concerts under the stars hit the beach in summer, while the adults-only Moorea Beach Club attracts sybaritic crowds by day with its DJs and topless sunbathing. What more could you desire?

For a roundup of Vegas' coolest adults-only pool parties and top-less poolside ultra lounges, see the boxed text (p154).

HIGHLIGHTS

>10 QUA BATHS & SPA

INDULGE IN BODILY BLISS AT A MODERN OASIS

Now more than ever, visiting Las Vegas is not merely about gambling. A stopover in Sin City these days is all about the headlong, hedonistic pursuit of pleasure in all its endless varieties, and so it was inevitable that fantastic, over-the-top spas would blossom like wildflowers here.

Seeking Hawaiian lomilomi, Japanese shiatsu or Thai massage? A volcanic mud or banana-leaf body wrap, a coconut-crème exfoliation? Or how about a lotus-flower bath or a soak in signature apothecary elixirs? At Caesars Palace, Qua Baths & Spa (p149) has everything you desire, and then some. Sweat out your hangover inside the aromatic cedar sauna. Take a dip in the Roman baths. Chill in the arctic room, where dry-ice snowflakes fall. Recline in the exotic-tea lounge, made for socializing with the girls. In the 'Men's Zone,' bad-boy poker players can get a royal shave or have their sore muscles kneaded just like victorious gladiators.

So, what are you waiting for? Treat yourself like an empress or emperor. For more highly recommended spas, see p147.

>11 STRATOSPHERE TOWER
GET HIGH OVER 100 STORIES ABOVE THE STRIP

After a long day traipsing up and down the Strip, especially when the dog days of summer make you sweat, there's no better heat relief than to whoosh up the Stratosphere Tower inside the USA's fastest elevators. There, almost 1150ft above the ground, strong winds make the city's air cooler, not to mention clearer. On a good day, it's a cinch to see for miles across the desert valley encircled by jagged mountains.

Whether you show up for sunset or star gazing, nothing tops this vista. Taking in the eagle's-eye city skyline will make you feel as rich as a high roller, especially as you knock back stiff martinis while listening to live jazz at the 107 Lounge (p132), or fork into a juicy steak at Top of the World restaurant (p115).

But those aren't the only ways to get high atop the Stratosphere Tower. At the pinnacle of the city's tallest building are some adrenaline-pumping thrill rides, including the aptly named Insanity, which swings riders out over the edge of the tower into thin air, then spins 'em round. Or try the brand-new SkyJump (p83), which really gets the blood rushing by letting you dive over the side of the spire in an 855ft controlled free fall. Whooh-hooh!

See p84 for more information.

>12 SPRINGS PRESERVE

DISCOVER REAL LIFE IN THE SOUTHERN NEVADA DESERT

Spread over 180 acres atop the site of the original springs and *las vegas* (the meadows), where Southern Paiute tribespeople and Old Spanish Trail traders once pitched their camps, and later Mormon missionaries and Western pioneers settled the Las Vegas Valley, this $250-million museum complex (p76) takes visitors on an incredible trip through historical, cultural and biological time.

If you want to dig beneath the hard-scrabble surface of this desert oasis, start with the Origen Experience. The 'Natural Mojave' galleries simulate flash floods and expose the variety of native wildlife that call this desert home, from Gila monsters to big brown bats. The 'People of the Springs' exhibit traces the city's obscure history, from Native American dwellings to the arrival of the railroad on the Western frontier and the construction of Hoover Dam. The 'New Frontier' rooms are stocked with kid-friendly interactive multimedia games that teach about conservation, the environment and life in the modern city. Who knew slot machines could be so educational?

The touchstone of the Springs Preserve is the forward-thinking Desert Living Center. Here, Nevada's first platinum-certified LEED

(Leadership in Energy and Environmental Design) buildings stand proudly, constructed of recycled materials and rammed-earth walls, with passive cooling, renewable heating, reclaimed water and solar-electricity panels, all harvesting clean energy. Inside the center are classrooms, learning labs and public exhibits designed to inspire visitors to consider the future of the Strip's neon jungle. The reality is, the sustainability of this fragile desert environment is a huge concern. We think Al Gore would agree – it's an inconvenient truth that can no longer be ignored.

Emerging from the main buildings, outdoor xeriscaped gardens flourish with over 30,000 plants.

Out back more than two miles of walking trails feature interpretive displays that piece together Nevada's cultural and natural history; bring along plenty of water and don't attempt to walk the trails in the blazing midday sun.

Afterward, stop by the nature-themed gift shop, which sells gifts, books, toys and brain-teaser souvenirs. Upstairs is the healthy, eco-conscious Springs Café by Wolfgang Puck. The Springs Preserve is also the future home of the Nevada State Museum, which should relocate here eventually.

For more about Las Vegas' 'green' outlook, see p173.

>13 YOUR HOTEL ROOM

HIDE OUT ALL WEEKEND LONG

Sometimes the best thing to do in Las Vegas is absolutely nothing at all – that is, if it's in the deluxe cocoon of your own hotel room or, better yet, a sweeter suite.

Sleeping in late is required for party animals who are out gambling and making merry mayhem till dawn. You'll find hotel rooms here have the most creative (and temptingly collectible) 'Do Not Disturb' signs: the ones at TI (Treasure Island) spell out 'inTImacy requested,' while the MGM Grand's West Wing simply says 'Recharging.'

There's very little that's not available in a minibar or on a room-service menu somewhere in this city. At the Hard Rock (p48), you can order Love Jones lingerie and erotic play boxes (with massage oils and…whoa, handcuffs!) delivered straight to your room. Buckets of champagne on ice are available at almost every casino hotel, but how many will deliver a $6000 combo meal of a burger, French fries and a vintage bottle of Bordeaux straight to your room like at the Palms (p55)?

The plushest casino hotels in Vegas (think Palazzo, Venetian, Wynn, Encore, Bellagio and MGM Grand) have exclusive all-suites towers staffed with VIP concierges to pamper you with any imaginable amenity, making sure you'll never want to leave.

For advice on where to stay, see p164.

Ship ahoy! The swashbuckling setting of TI (Treasure Island; p61)

ITINERARIES

Although the house always has an edge in Las Vegas, it's a sure bet that there is more to do on the Strip, in downtown and all around town than you'll have time to spare, so make every second count. These high-voltage itineraries will help you get started, fast.

ONE DAY

Speed from the airport to the Strip. Check in at your hotel resort, or just drop off your bags, then go straight to the gaming tables. Take in the Strip's fabulous free attractions (p80) and shopping arcades (p92) as you stroll through opulent megaresorts (p32) such as Aria, the Bellagio, Caesars Palace, Venetian, Palazzo, Wynn and Encore. Use the monorail (p190) or Ace and Deuce buses (p190) to roll up and down Las Vegas Blvd. Dine at a top chef's table (see the boxed text, p104), then party at Sin City's hottest bars (p132) and nightclubs (p140) until the sun comes up. After a quick cat nap, hit a big buffet (p171) before catching your flight out.

ONE WEEKEND

Fly into Vegas on Friday. Follow the one-day itinerary, but without rushing around like such a crazy person. Fire up your first night at the Strip's ultra lounges (p152) and wind it down around dawn at an after-hours hot spot (p152).

Sleep late the next morning. Laze by the pool (p154), take a gambling lesson or indulge at a primo spa (p147). Get your kicks atop the Stratosphere Tower (p23) as the sun sinks below the horizon, then head downtown to neon-lit Glitter Gulch or boomerang right back to the Strip.

Wake up to an indulgent Sunday brunch (see the boxed text, p126), then gamble or shop like mad until the last minute (even at the airport).

THREE DAYS

Do everything we've recommended in the one-day and one-weekend itineraries. Make time for a trip out of town, too, to either the awe-inspiring Grand Canyon (p156) or nearby Hoover Dam (p158), followed by a scenic drive around Lake Mead (p158) and the Valley of Fire (p158).

Left The crowds snap away while the big cats slumber at MGM Grand's lion habitat (p77)

On your last day, stop by a half-price ticket booth (see the boxed text, p131) for tickets to a comedy or magic act (p138) or, if you're lucky, a knock-out stage show (p144). In the afternoon, detour off the beaten tourist path to the Springs Preserve (p24), Atomic Testing Museum (p15) or downtown's fun, funky 18b Arts District (p14).

COMP CITY
When you're down to the felt (ie on your last dime), don't despair. Some of Las Vegas' best diversions don't cost a thing. Popular low-roller attractions include the Bellagio's dancing fountains (p80), the Mirage's exploding volcano (p81), the Sirens of TI pirate battle at Treasure Island (p81), the MGM Grand's lion habitat (p77), the Flamingo's tropical wildlife gardens (p77), high-wire circus acts at Circus Circus (p80) and celebrity impersonators inside the Imperial Palace casino (p78). Downtown has the unabashedly tacky Fremont Street Experience (p80), while raucous First Friday (p14) block parties happen in the nearby 18b Arts District. Venture east of the Strip to the Hard Rock casino (p48), where priceless rock 'n' roll memorabilia adorns the walls.

HIGH ROLLERS
Cruise the Strip in a cherry-red convertible and hit the high-stakes poker tables for a taste of James Bond–style action. After sunset, dine with a powerhouse chef (see the boxed text, p104), then mingle with Hollywood

Flash the cash at the upmarket Forum Shops (p92)

FORWARD PLANNING

One to six months before you go Book your flights (p188) and accommodations (p164). If you'll be taking any trips out of town (p155), reserve a rental car (p190).

Three to four weeks before you go Start surfing key Las Vegas websites (p192) and dabbling in the local media (p193); score tickets for any major concerts, production shows or sporting events that catch your eye (see the boxed text, p151) or reserve an out-of-town adventure tour (p161); book a table at a star chef's restaurant (p101).

A week before you go Call your hotel (p164) to check if room prices have dropped and if so, request that your reservation rate be lowered, too – you could save hundreds of dollars that way. Make an appointment at one of the Strip's lavish unisex spas (p147).

The day before you go Reconfirm your flight, hotel and car-rental reservations, and print out copies of everything. Check local blogs (p192), Twitter and Facebook community pages for late-breaking news about the hottest nightclubs and live entertainment, then sign up for mobile phone text offers (p191) from casino hotels.

celebrities at a sultry ultra lounge (p152) and party till dawn in a nightclub's VIP room (p140). Wake up around noon the next day. Start off with a champagne buffet (p171), then soak up the desert sun by a sexy pool lounge (p154) or luxuriate at a spa (p147). Take your photo standing next to a million-dollar sportscar at the Ferrari Maserati dealership showroom at Wynn (p63) after bagging the latest fashions from New York, Los Angeles, Milan, Paris and Tokyo inside the Strip's megaresort malls (p92).

ALTERNATIVE VEGAS

When you've tired of the Strip's neon nights, the flip side of Las Vegas beckons. East of Fremont St's casino row is downtown's break-out entertainment district, anchored by the indie Beauty Bar (p134), hepcats' Griffin (p135) and plush Downtown Cocktail Room (p134). During daylight hours, wander the 18b Arts District (p14), full of creative art galleries (p74), vintage clothing and antiques shops (p88), and only-in-Vegas stores (p99). Find refreshment at locals' fave Luv-It Frozen Custard (p120), then go green at the inspiring Springs Preserve (p24), with its top-notch museum, interpretive trails and gardens, or get a blast of Nevada's atomic past at the Atomic Testing Museum (p15). For sheer silliness, drop by the Pinball Hall of Fame (p79). Time your visit for a First Friday (p14) block party in the 18b Arts District or a local festival (p132).

>CASINOS & GAMBLING

Take a chance on Lady Luck in Las Vegas

CASINOS & GAMBLING

You're on your umpteenth martini. You've just won big the last three hands. Adrenaline pumping, you double down – and lose half of your piggy bank. It's all part of the Vegas experience, and the thrill of hitting the jackpot (no matter how unlikely) is why so many people keep coming back.

It's important to remember one thing: the house advantage. In every game except poker, the house has a statistical winning edge (the 'percentage') over the gambler, and for nearly every payout in nearly every game, the house 'holds' a small portion of the winnings. Amounts vary with the game and with individual bets, but over the long haul, you're guaranteed to lose everything that you gamble. Have fun, but understand the games you're playing, don't bet more than you're prepared to lose, and learn to leave when you're 'up' (ahead).

Traditional casino games include poker, blackjack, baccarat, craps, roulette and slot machines. You must be at least 21 years old to play or even hang around in a casino. Every game has its own customs, traditions and strategies. Almost all casinos hand out written guides to show how to play the game and may offer free one-hour lessons in table games, from Texas Hold'em and blackjack to dice-rollin' craps, all taught by pros. It's OK to ask your dealer for help and advice. For instance, the dealer can tell you what the strategy is for the blackjack hand you've just been dealt. It's polite to 'toke' (tip) the dealer if you are winning. Either place a chip on the layout (the area where you place your bet) for the dealer to take, or place a side bet for the dealer to collect if it wins.

If you play table games seriously, ask the pit boss to rate your play, based on how much you bet and how many hours you play. Las Vegas

---

Top left Why sit barside at the Flamingo (p46) when you can nurse your drink in the pool? **Top right** Dress to impress at The Bank (p142) at Bellagio **Bottom** Do your best to imitate the good-luck statues at Harrah's (p66)

casinos give out millions of dollars in 'comps' to rated players (unrated players get nothing) every year.

Even if you're only betting $5 to $10 per hand, you could earn yourself a free buffet pass. Table-game, slot-machine and video-poker players all earn comps by signing up for casinos' players'

> **BEST CASINOS FOR HIGH-LIMIT GAMING**
> > Bellagio (p42)
> > Mansion at MGM Grand (p51)
> > Mirage (p52)
> > Venetian (p62)
> > Wynn (p63)

clubs. Membership is free, but you must be at least 21 years old and have photo ID. Just go to the players' club desk or the cashier's cage inside the casino and ask to join. You'll have your players' club card – plus a free souvenir T-shirt, two-for-one drinks coupon, $10 in free slot play or other token welcome gift – within minutes.

POKER

Poker has become the hottest game in town. Fueled by seemingly endless TV coverage and the explosion of online play, would-be legends are flocking to the tables, ready to test their cunning and grit against other hometown heroes and touring pros. Hit a big-league poker room at the wrong time on a Friday night, and you may be in for a three-hour wait just to sit down. Newer, flashier poker rooms have electronic signboards and hand out pagers to notify you when your seat is available. Nonsmoking rooms are catching on, too.

Many poker rooms take only a small percentage of each pot, leaving the vast majority of the money to be won and lost by the players themselves. Poker betting comes in three basic flavors: limit, no limit and pot limit. While it's not the only game in town, Texas Hold'em (p175) is far and away the most common. Novices can pick up a strategy book or two from the Gamblers Book Shop (p90).

BLACKJACK

While poker may be grabbing the headlines, blackjack (aka '21') remains far and away the most popular table game Vegas has to offer. Players love blackjack for all kinds of reasons. It's relatively simple to master its basic strategies, and there's easy camaraderie with sociable dealers. Almost every player has had the experience of making an absolute killing at the table, leading them to feel blackjack is a 'beatable' game. But not all blackjack games are created equal, and every casino lays down its own set of rules. Avoid games that won't allow you to split aces or that pay 6:5 odds instead of the usual 3:2.

Nearly all blackjack strategies revolve around one basic fact: because so many cards have a value of 10 – the tens, jacks, queens and kings make up nearly a third of the deck – it's usually good practice to assume that any unknown card, ie the dealer's hole card or the card you are thinking about hitting for, is going to be worth 10. Many gift shops in Las Vegas casino hotels sell little plastic cards telling you what your most advantageous play is in each situation, and friendly dealers will offer you the same advice.

BACCARAT

Nothing conjures the image of high stakes, black tuxedos and James Bond like baccarat, and yet, of the card games, it possesses the least strategy – none, in fact. The rules of the game are fixed, and there are no decisions for the player except for how to bet. High minimum bets ensure that only those with large bankrolls sit down to play. However, you may be able to find a few mini baccarat tables with $5 minimum bets.

CRAPS

A lively and fast-paced craps table has players shouting, crowds gathering and everyone hoping for that lucky 'hot' streak of the dice. Even

---

BEST BETS FOR PLAYERS

> Blackjack – Rules vary from table to table, but check out low-roller casinos downtown and on the North Strip.
> Craps – The odds may change, but good times roll at the Strip's Casino Royale, downtown's Main Street Station and Sam's Town off-Strip.
> Race and sports books – Hilton has the world's largest, but Wynn, Caesars Palace and the MGM Grand impress; Palazzo's Lagasse Stadium has gourmet grub.
> Roulette – Paris Las Vegas and a few high-limit gaming salons on the Strip have authentic European wheels, which improves your odds of winning.
> Video poker – The Palms, west of the Strip, and some downtown casino hotels have full-pay machines.

though the odds are exactly the same on every roll, that doesn't stop people from betting their 'hunches' and believing that certain numbers are 'due.'

Because the betting possibilities are complicated, and shift as play continues, it's important to spend some time studying a betting guide and begin playing with the simplest wager, on the pass/don't pass line, which also happens to be one of the better bets in a Vegas casino.

ROULETTE

The ancient game of roulette is easy to understand and hypnotic to play. Roulette provides the clearest demonstration of the house edge. The roulette wheel has 38 numbers – from 1 to 36, plus 0 and 00 (European roulette wheels typically do not have '00,' which makes the American version much harder). The layout of the wheel is marked with the numbers and various betting combinations.

Most bets pay off at even money, but the chances of a win are less than 50%, because the 0 and 00 don't count as odd or even, red or black, high or low. These aren't the best odds in the casino, but they're far from the worst.

SPEAK LIKE A GAMBLING SAVANT
all in – to bet everything you've got
ante – a starting wager required to play table games
comps – freebies (eg buffet passes, show tickets, hotel rooms) given to players
cooler – an unlucky gambler who makes everyone else lose
dealertainer – a card dealer with an act (eg impersonating Billy Idol)
eye in the sky – high-tech casino surveillance systems
fold – to throw in your cards and stop betting
high roller – a gambler who bets big (aka 'whale')
let it ride – to roll over a winning wager into the next bet
low roller – a small-time gambler (eg likes 1¢ slot machines)
marker – IOU credit-line debt owed to a casino
one-armed bandit – old-fashioned nickname for a slot machine
pit boss – a card dealer's supervisor on the casino floor
sucker bet – a gamble on nearly impossible odds
toke – a tip or gratuity

SLOT MACHINES & VIDEO POKER

Simplest of all are slot machines – just put in money and pull the handle (or push a button) – and they're wildly popular. A player can have no effect on the outcome. The probabilities are programmed into the machine, and the chances of winning (or more likely losing) are the same on every pull.

Some machines pay back a higher proportion of the money deposited than others; those with larger-than-average returns (up to 98%) are called 'loose.'

If you hit the jackpot, always wait by the machine until an attendant arrives, so you can claim your prize.

Popular with locals, video poker games are often built into a bar. By employing correct strategy (math whizzes can memorize strategy tables) and finding machines with the best payout schedules, it's possible to improve your chances of winning.

Look for machines that reward a pair of jacks or better, and have a one-coin payout of nine coins for a full house and six coins for a flush (ie a 9/6 Jacks or Better machine).

SPORTS BOOKS

The bigger casinos usually have a race and sports book, a room where major sports events are televised. Players can bet on just about any game, boxing match or horse race in the country, except for those taking place in Nevada.

Race and sports books are best during major events, when everyone is captivated by, betting on and yelling about the same thing, such as NFL Monday Night Football, college basketball's March Madness and pro baseball's World Series.

MAJOR PLAYERS & GAMBLING-HALL FAVES

Las Vegas literally has scores of casinos, all offering different games and odds.

The following pages describe major players on Las Vegas Blvd and downtown's Fremont St, plus a few other gambling-hall faves, both on and off the Strip. All are open 24 hours, don't charge admission, are wheelchair-accessible and offer free self-service and valet parking (tip at least $2).

ARIA

Forget about kitsch. Las Vegas is all grown up now, with towering new luxury playgrounds offering more urbane experiences. Take, for example, MGM Mirage's CityCenter complex, whose spiring boutique hotels and high-minded public artwork have transformed both the skyline and landscape of the Strip.

Believe it or not, there's only one casino at CityCenter. And that's at **Aria** (☎ 590-7111; www.arialasvegas.com; 🚌 Deuce), a resort hotel with a Japanese-inspired spa, heavy-hitter dining rooms (p104) and a quirky Cirque du Soleil show, *Viva Elvis* (p147), which has its own official store (p98) for die-hard fans of the King.

Beside Aria, CityCenter's Crystals mall (p92) is another LEED gold-certified building, dazzling passersby with a three-story interior 'tree-house,' high-tech water and ice sculptures, and a glass canopy jutting out from high-fashion designer shops onto the Strip.

The nearby Mandarin Oriental hotel is a five-star hideaway. Don't let the doormen deter you, however: anyone is welcome to take the elevators up to the 23rd-floor 'Sky Lobby,' where floor-to-ceiling windows allow glittering Strip views, best enjoyed with a cocktail from Mandarin Bar & Tea Lounge (p136) or at Twist by Pierre Gagnaire (p105), a posh French restaurant.

Free trams shuttle between the Monte Carlo and Bellagio casino hotels, stopping at CityCenter.

Glittering Aria adds even more razzle-dazzle to the Strip

Jasmine Freeman
Poker player & card dealer at the M Resort

How did you get started dealing? I used to have a 'normal' job and I'd just come in to play poker, have fun and relax. Dealers get paid to play a game all day. I thought, 'Why not?' **What do you love about your job?** Every day is different. When you're dealing with people, you never know what you're walking into. **What makes a good card dealer?** Being tough-skinned. **Advice for women poker players?** Show your confidence. Some men feel they understand male players, but not how women think. That can be an advantage. **Tips for newbies?** Start at poker tables with lower limits and get experience without blowing your whole bankroll. You can play more, and you can play longer. **What's the best and most challenging thing about living in Vegas?** There's so much to do – this city is open 24 hours. I have to remember to schedule time to sleep.

BELLAGIO

Built by Steve Wynn on the site of the legendary Dunes, the **Bellagio** (☎ 693-7111; www.bellagio.com; 3600 Las Vegas Blvd S; Ⓜ Bally's/Paris) is Vegas' original, opulent, if entirely parvenu, pleasure villa. You may recognize it from the 2001 remake of the Rat Pack–era movie *Ocean's Eleven*. At the water's edge of an artificial lake, from which spring more than a thousand dancing fountains (p80), is a cluster of Tuscan buildings purporting the illusion of having been plucked from Italy's Lake District.

Although the nouveau-riche stink can be heady, the secret delight of the Bellagio is that romance is always in the air, and natural light swathes plenty of private nooks where you can soak up the atmosphere. Beyond the glass-and-metal *porte cochere* you'll find a stable of high-end restaurants (p102), a swish shopping concourse (p94), a fine-art gallery (p74) and a European-style casino.

The hotel's gasp-worthy lobby is adorned with Dale Chihuly's glass sculpture composed of 2000 hand-blown flowers in vibrant colors. Real flowers, cultivated in a gigantic on-site greenhouse, brighten countless vases throughout the property and an over-the-top conservatory (p77). In the courtyard, a swimming pool is accented by carved Italian columns and manicured citrus and parterre gardens.

Unaccompanied children under 18 are not allowed at the Bellagio. Baby strollers are prohibited except for use by hotel guests.

The stately exterior of the Bellagio

CAESARS PALACE

As showcased in the Hollywood film *Rain Man*, **Caesars Palace** (☎ 731-7110; www.caesarspalace.com; 3570 Las Vegas Blvd S; Ⓜ Flamingo/Caesars Palace) upped the luxury ante for the gaming industry when it debuted in the 1960s. The Greco-Roman fantasyland captured the world's attention with its full-sized marble reproductions of classical statuary, its Stripside row of towering fountains and its cocktail waitresses costumed as goddesses.

Thanks to ongoing megabucks renovations, Caesars is redefining its swanky self. At the sybaritic Garden of the Gods Oasis pool complex, hotties proffer frozen grapes in summer, and topless sunbathing is allowed at Venus Pool Club. Pure (p143) is a celeb-happy nightclub, while crooner Matt Goss brings the paparazzi to Cleopatra's Barge.

Although Caesars appears poised to rule the empire once again, the Palace remains quintessentially kitschy Vegas. Bar girls continue to roam the gaming areas in skimpy togas, and the fountains are still out front – the same ones daredevil Evil Knievel made famous when he jumped them on a motorcycle on December 31, 1967.

Two imperial casinos contain more than 100 card tables and a couple of thousand slots that will accept up to $500 chips, as well as a race and sports book with giant TV screens. Fashionistas saunter inside the upscale Forum Shops (p92), which feature an aquarium and bizarre animatronic fountain shows. The Colosseum, a 4100-seat showroom modeled after its Roman namesake, puts on lavish theatrical spectacles. Also found here is a galaxy of star chefs' restaurants (p103).

Bask in the lap of luxury at Caesars Palace

CIRCUS CIRCUS

While cruising the bedraggled North Strip, it's pretty hard to miss **Circus Circus** (☎ 734-0410; www.circuscircus.com; 2880 Las Vegas Blvd S; 🚍 Deuce), what with its enormous clown-shaped marquee and tent-shaped casino under a gaudily striped big top. From the outside, this sprawling resort may look pretty cheesy – and it definitely *is*. It's also overrun with kiddies and baby strollers.

Open since 1968, this casino hotel was originally intended to stand beside Caesars Palace; that way, it could've had a Roman circus theme. But that wasn't meant to be, so now it's just a plain circus here. The decor is a riotous carnival of colors, mainly pinks and oranges, that aims for Ringling Bros more than *commedia dell'arte*. A trio of full-sized casinos have over 2200 slot machines (keep an eye out for those spinning carousels), plus zany table games like 'Casino War.'

If you're a wild child yourself, relive scenes from Hunter S Thompson's gonzo journalism epic *Fear and Loathing in Las Vegas: A Savage Journey to the Heart of the American Dream* here, but even without the drugs it's hallucinogenic enough. Elevated above the casino floor, trapeze artists, high-wire workers, jugglers and unicyclists perform stunts (p80), while out back is the Adventuredome amusement park (p81). Cacophonous Slots A' Fun (p80) is just a drunken stumble away.

Rediscover your inner child at Circus Circus

EXCALIBUR

Arthurian legends notwithstanding, this medieval caricature, complete with crayon-colored towers and a faux drawbridge, epitomizes gaudy Vegas. **Excalibur** (☎ 597-7777; www.excalibur.com; 3850 Las Vegas Blvd S; M MGM Grand) could have resembled an elegant English castle, but its designers decided to go the kitschy route instead, which is just fine with the cheapskate frat boys and families with rambunctious young kids who stay here.

Inside the inane mock-castle, the casino walls are hung with coats of arms and cheap stained-glass art imitations that depict valiant knights and lovely damsels. Down on the Fantasy Faire Midway are buried Ye Olde carnival games like skee-ball, and there are joystick joys and Merlin's Magic Motion Machine ridefilms in the Wizard's Arcade. For kids, the *Tournament of Kings* dinner show is a demolition derby with hooves and sticky fingers.

Excalibur is handily connected to Luxor by an underground moving walkway. A free tram also links Excalibur, Luxor and Mandalay Bay.

Experience a taste of medieval times at Excalibur

FLAMINGO

In 1946 the **Flamingo** (☎ 733-3111; www.flamingolasvegas.com; 3555 Las Vegas Blvd S; Ⓜ Flamingo/Caesars Palace) was the talk of the town. The New York Mafia had shelled out millions to finish building this tropical gaming oasis in the desert. Billy Wilkerson, owner of the *Hollywood Reporter* and some sizzling-hot LA nightclubs, originally broke ground here. But he ran out of money fast, so the mob stepped in.

It was prime gangster Americana, initially managed by the infamous mobster Benjamin 'Bugsy' Siegel, who named it after his girlfriend, dancer Virginia Hill, called 'The Flamingo' for her red hair and long legs. Siegel died in a hail of bullets at Hill's Beverly Hills bungalow soon after the Flamingo opened, the victim of a contract killing. The Flamingo had gotten off to a rocky start and the investors mistakenly believed it would ultimately fail, so they 'took care of business.' But they were so wrong: not only did the Flamingo survive, it kick-started modern Las Vegas and the entire Strip.

Today, the Flamingo isn't quite what it was back when its janitorial staff wore tuxedos; think more *Miami Vice*, less *Bugsy*. But it's always crowded in the casino. Drop by during the madhouse sunset happy hour to sling back margaritas in souvenir glasses and watch women of questionable repute stroll past the front doors. Bugsy would've loved it.

Soak up the retro atmosphere at Flamingo

GOLDEN NUGGET

The Golden Nugget's namesake claim to fame is the Hand of Faith. (No, it's not a religious relic.) It's the heftiest hunk of gold ever found, weighing a massive 61lb 11oz. Discovered in Australia, today it's on display under glass near the North Tower elevators. Yet that's not all this bejeweled gambling palace is known for.

When it debuted as the world's largest casino in 1946, the **Golden Nugget** (☎ 385-7111; www.goldennugget.com; 129 E Fremont St; 🚌 Ace Gold, Deuce) looked like a million bucks and, unbelievably, poker players were allowed to deal their own cards. In the 1970s, casino impresario Steve Wynn brought vintage Vegas back into style by inviting Frank Sinatra to star. In the 21st century the Nugget was catapulted into the national limelight by the Fox reality-TV series *Casino*.

Day or night, the Nugget is downtown's most glam address, although the crowds of polyester-clad retirees are the antithesis of hip. The glittering casino has a spread of slots and table games, notably a nonsmoking poker room. Live bands rock the Rush Lounge, old-school steaks are served at Vic & Anthony's (p121) and Italian pizzas are wood-fired at the Grotto (p120). Reserved for hotel guests, a three-story water slide thrillingly plunges through a 200,000-gallon shark tank into a swimming pool outside. In the high-rise Rush Tower, Chart House seafood restaurant (p119) encircles an enormous tropical-fish aquarium.

Slide through a shark tank at the Golden Nugget and live to tell the tale

HARD ROCK

The world's first rock 'n' roll casino, the hot, hot, hot **Hard Rock** (☎ 693-5000; www.hardrockhotel.com; 4455 Paradise Rd; 🚌 108) embraces what may be the most impressive collection of rock-star memorabilia ever assembled under one roof. Among the priceless items being watched over by the 'eye in the sky' and eagle-eyed security guards suited up like bouncers are some of the more bodacious fashion statements by Elvis and Britney Spears; a custom motorcycle (donated by Nikki Sixx of Mötley Crüe) that once belonged to the Hell's Angels gang; and Jim Morrison's handwritten lyrics to one of The Doors' greatest hits.

All in all, this sexy, see-and-be-seen scene is perfect for entourage wannabes, and is especially beloved by SoCal partiers. A newly expanded casino has blackjack tables with Hell's Belles go-go dancers. Nearby are the Joint by Rogue concert venue (p140), Vanity nightclub (p144), edgy boutique shops (p93) and Reliquary Water Sanctuary & Spa. There's seasonal swim-up blackjack at the Beach Club, open to the public for Rehab pool parties (see the boxed text, p154) on summer Sundays.

Like a shot of Viagra, the Hard Rock's glam Tower Suites and SkyBar pool lounge have only enhanced the potency of its forever-young appeal.

Take a tour through rock 'n' roll history at the Hard Rock

LUXOR

Named after Egypt's ancient city perched on the east bank of the Nile, the landmark **Luxor** (☎ 262-4000; www.luxor.com; 3900 Las Vegas Blvd S; 🚍 Deuce) once had the biggest 'wow!' factor of the South Strip's megaresorts. It tenuously hung in the balance between being a pyramid of gaudiness and a refined shrine to Egyptian art, architecture and antiquities. All that kitsch is now going the way of the pharaohs, as a brash North African theme is replaced with sexed-up nightlife (p153) and contempo restaurants (p107).

Fronting the 30-story pyramid cloaked in black glass from base to apex are a crouching sphinx and a sandstone obelisk etched with hieroglyphics. For now, the pyramid's interior is stuffed full of enormous Egyptian statues of guards, lions and rams; sandstone columns and walls adorned with tapestries; a stunning replica of the Great Temple of Ramses II; and a pharaoh's treasure of polished marble. The hotel atrium is so voluminous it could fit nine Boeing 747s stacked on top of one another. At the apex of the pyramid, a 40-billion-candlepower beacon, the world's most powerful, sends a shaft of bluish-white light 10 miles out into space, where it's visible by astronauts.

The Luxor is linked to Excalibur by an underground moving walkway. To get to Mandalay Bay, walk through Mandalay Place mall (p93). A free tram also connects Luxor with Mandalay Bay and Excalibur.

Walk like an Egyptian at Luxor

MANDALAY BAY

The tropical-themed **'M-Bay'** (☎ 632-7777; www.mandalaybay.com; 3950 Las Vegas Blvd S; 🚌 Deuce) fails to match the grandeur of Vegas' more famous mega-resorts, although high-stakes gamblers will appreciate a classy casino that seems as limitless as the credit line needed to play here. Everything can be a spectacle here, if you only know where to look.

Big-name bands electrify the House of Blues (p140) and M-Bay's events center (see the boxed text, p151), catsuit-clad 'angels' scale the wine tower at Aureole (p107), and sable fur coats are loaned to enter the frozen vodka locker inside Red Square. Stylish boutique extras include Mandalay Place (p93), a skybridge shopping promenade, and the minimalist modern THEhotel with its lofty Mix bar (p137) and bathhouse spa (p148).

M-Bay's aquatic theme hinges on the Shark Reef (p78), an awesome glassed-in, walk-through aquarium; and the artificial Mandalay Beach, built with 2700 tons of imported Californian sand, featuring summer 'dive-in' movies, surfing competitions in an artificial wave pool, starlight concerts by rock 'n' roll legends and topless Moorea Beach Club. If the stress of gambling in the air-con beachside casino gets to be too much, retire to a rooftop cabana or float away on a lazy river ride.

Free trams shuttle between Mandalay Bay and the Luxor and Excalibur casino hotels.

Rock out to live music at the House of Blues, Mandalay Bay

MGM GRAND

With over 5040 rooms, **MGM Grand** (☎ 891-1111; www.mgmgrand.com; 3799 Las Vegas Blvd S; M MGM Grand) held the 'world's largest hotel' crown until just recently. Astoundingly, the resort contains no fewer than 18,000 doors, 7778 beds and 93 elevators. The important thing to remember is that despite its enormous size, the shimmering emerald-green 'City of Entertainment' – looking like something straight out of *The Wizard of Oz* – manages to feel intimate, even clubby.

Formerly owned by movie corp Metro Goldwyn Mayer, the MGM has co-opted themes from Hollywood movies, down to the black-and-white photos of yesteryear's film stars hanging in the restrooms. The casino consists of a gigantic, circular room with a domed ceiling and replicated 1930s glamour. The gaming area is equal in size to four football fields and offers a whopping selection of slots and table games, plus a hot poker room next to a race and sports book with VIP skyboxes.

Out front, it's hard to miss the USA's largest bronze statue, a 100,000lb lion that's 45ft tall, perched atop a pedestal ringed by fountains and Atlas-themed statues. More 'Maximum Vegas' attractions include the lion habitat (p77), the gigantic MGM Grand Garden Arena (see the boxed text, p151), which hosts championship boxing bouts and concerts, Cirque du Soleil's martial-arts-inspired show *Kà* (p145), the topless revue Crazy Horse Paris (p145) and a celebrity-chef lineup (p108).

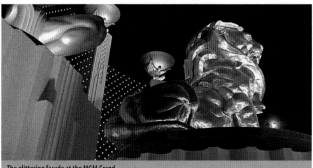
The glittering facade at the MGM Grand

MIRAGE

Despite having been open for more than 20 years, there's still nothing quite like casino mogul Steve Wynn's most exotic creation, **Mirage** (☎ 791-7111; www.mirage.com; 3400 Las Vegas Blvd S; Ⓜ Harrah's/Imperial Palace). Its paradisiacal tropical setting, replete with an atrium of jungle foliage and waterfalls (p78), captures the imagination. Out front in a lagoon, the fiery trademark faux volcano (p81) erupts nightly, stopping slack-jawed onlookers in their tracks.

The scents of jasmine and vanilla often waft through the hotel lobby. Circling the atrium is a huge Polynesian-themed casino, which incorporates the design concept of placing gaming areas under separate roofs to invoke a feeling of intimacy. Real and faux tropical plants add to the splendor of the casino, which has a high-stakes poker room.

Until recently the Mirage was outstripped by the Strip's newer, splashier megaresorts, including Steve Wynn's eponymous resort up the street. But the Mirage has recently climbed back toward the top of the Strip game by adding a smash-hit Cirque du Soleil show, *LOVE* (p146); the Beatles-themed Revolution Lounge (p153); a hot nightclub, Jet (p142); Caribbean-cool Rhumbar (p137); an adults-only pool lounge, Bare (see the boxed text, p154); and crowd-pleasing eateries (p109).

Although the dynamic duo is no longer performing here, you can still visit Siegfried & Roy's Secret Garden & Dolphin Habitat (p78), then pay your respects to the giant shrine-like bronze statue of the legendary illusionists standing outside on the Strip.

Gaze at the underwater world in the Mirage lobby

*702 . 11 AM -

NEW YORK–NEW YORK

Give me your tired, huddled (over a Wheel of Fortune slot machine) masses. The mini-megapolis of **New York–New York** (☎ 740-6969; www.nyny hotelcasino.com; 3790 Las Vegas Blvd S; Ⓜ MGM Grand) has scaled-down replicas of the Empire State Building and Statue of Liberty, a mini Brooklyn Bridge and scale-warped renditions of the Chrysler and Ziggurat buildings, all topped off by a roller coaster (p82) wrapped around the colorful facade. The crowd is young and party-hardy.

Zany design elements throughout reflect NYC's bold color, history and diversity. Don't overlook the USA bas-relief map at America coffee shop or Greenwich Village's cobblestone streets. Claustrophobes, beware. This Disneyfied version of the Big Apple can get more crowded than the real deal: around 200,000 pedestrians stride across NYC's Brooklyn Bridge each year, but around 15 million traverse the Vegas version annually.

Slews of slots and gaming tables are set against a rich backdrop of famous landmarks, with high-limit 'Gaming on the Green.' The Bar at Times Square (p133) is famous for its dueling piano acts. Sip a more civilized pint outdoors at Nine Fine Irishmen (see the boxed text, p136), where live Celtic bands play, or taste North American microbrews at Pour 24 (see the boxed text, p136). Kids gravitate to the Coney Island Emporium (p82), a high-tech video and virtual-reality game arcade upstairs by the roller coaster.

Learn a trick or two at Houdini's Magic Shop, New York–New York

PALAZZO

A grandiose sequel to the Venetian (p62), the **Palazzo** (☎ 607-7777; www
.palazzolasvegas.com; 3325 Las Vegas Blvd S; M Harrah's/Imperial Palace) casino resort
opened opposite Wynn with great fanfare in 2008. This upscale casino
hotel was supposed to have been called Lido, after the Italian island just
a short boat ride away from Venice at the edge of the Adriatic Sea. Here
in Las Vegas, you can walk from Venice to its offshore island in just a few
minutes.

The Venetian and Palazzo resorts are connected via an interior corridor.
Entering the Palazzo, you'll emerge into an airy, sunshine-filled atrium
with a waterfall feature, a fave photo op for camera-toting tourists.
Soaring 50 floors toward the sky, the Palazzo's all-suites hotel tower is
one of the Strip's tallest. The casino itself measures over 100,000 sq ft,
with the usual spread of high-limit table games and slot and video-poker
machines with less-favorable odds.

At the Shoppes at the Palazzo (p94), international designers flaunt
their goodies, while the Canyon Ranch SpaClub induces aqua-thermal
bliss. High-flying restaurants (p111) include exhilarating ventures by
culinary heavyweights Emeril Legasse and Wolfgang Puck.

Stroll fountainside at the Palazzo

PALMS

Designed to seduce Gen-Xers and Gen-Yers, the ultramodern **Palms** (☎ 942-7777; www.palms.com; 4321 W Flamingo Rd; 🚌 202) catapulted into the limelight with a starring role on MTV's *Real World* reality-TV series and Bravo's *Celebrity Poker Showdown*. Today it's Hugh Hefner's Playboy Club that calls the shots, and you'll have to cough up some cash to peek inside his hybrid casino-nightspot atop the Palms' Fantasy Tower, where flashy Moon nightclub (p143) has a retractable roof that opens up to the desert's starry skies.

Downstairs the high-drama, neon-lit atmosphere is equal parts sexy and downright cheesy – just like the Playboy bunnies upstairs. The main casino has quick cocktail service and a heavenly spread of full-pay video poker machines, plus two poker rooms and a race and sports book with interactive TVs and specialty wagering. The first-rate movie theater (p137) hosts the CineVegas film festival (p132).

Other places to see and be seen include Hart & Huntington Tattoo Shop, with its blood-red curtained fortune teller's booth out front; N9NE steakhouse (p127) and towering Alizé (p125) and Nove Italiano (p127) restaurants; ghostbar (p153), a sky-high ultra lounge that packs in celebs; and The Pearl (p140), a state-of-the-art concert hall and recording studio.

The Palms has upped the ante with Palms Place, a high-rise condo-hotel next door, where you can cure your hangover inside Drift Spa & Hammam (p148).

Imbibe a martini or three at the Palms

PARIS LAS VEGAS

Adorned with fake Francophonic signs such as 'Le Car Rental,' the multimillion-dollar Gallic caricature **Paris Las Vegas** (☎ 946-7000; www.paris lasvegas.com; 3655 Las Vegas Blvd S; Ⓜ Bally's/Paris) strives to evoke the gaiety of the grand dame by re-creating her famous landmarks, including the Paris Opera House, Arc de Triomphe, Hotel de Ville, Louvre and River Seine. Just like in the French capital, the signature attraction is the ersatz Eiffel Tower (p82), where visitors can ascend in a glass elevator to a head-spinning observation platform overlooking the Strip.

Surrounded by street scenes from both banks of the Seine, the bustling vault-ceilinged casino, complete with replica Métropolitain arches, is home to almost a hundred gaming tables, a couple of thousand slot machines, a race and sports book and some of the USA's only authentic French roulette wheels (which have no '00') in the high-limit area. Cracked crab legs are waiting on ice over at Le Village Buffet (p113), not far from the savory-and-sweet La Creperie.

Paris is conveniently connected to Bally's monorail station by a petite shopping arcade, where high heels clack along cobblestone streets.

Magnifique! The grounds of Paris Las Vegas

PLANET HOLLYWOOD

In a slightly out-of-the-way locale, **Planet Hollywood** (☎ 785-5555; www.planet hollywoodresort.com; 3667 Las Vegas Blvd S; Ⓜ Bally's/Paris) took its sweet time stripping the ex–Aladdin casino hotel of all of the trappings of its Middle Eastern fantasy. For fans of vintage Vegas, that felt like a crime. But for Paris Hilton imitators, World Series of Poker wannabes and those who like their casinos pimped out in LA style, the new PH fits the bill.

Dating from the 1950s, the original Aladdin, where Elvis and Priscilla Presley married, was imploded in 1998. Retooled to target the Asian and European jet set, the new Aladdin megaresort opened its doors just two years later. Quickly thereafter the owners made the largest bankruptcy filing ever in Nevada history. Some pundits even speculated the property was hexed.

The Aladdin's *new* new owners, Harrah's, have not dramatically changed this megaresort yet. For now, the genie's latest masters have kept a few of the Aladdin's gold-star attractions, including tastebud ticklers like the Spice Market Buffet (p114), Koi sushi bar (p114) and bordello-esque Strip House (p114) for steaks.

But don't hold your breath: no one has ever made a mint with this property – not yet, anyway. Your best bet is shopping at the adjacent Miracle Mile Shops (p94), formerly Desert Passage, and partying after-hours at Krāve nightclub (p142).

Go the distance at Planet Hollywood's Miracle Mile Shops

RIO

The name of this wildly popular casino hotel says a lot about the **Rio** (☎ 777-7777; www.riolasvegas.com; 3700 W Flamingo Rd; 🚌 free Strip shuttle). The corny Masquerade Village, the center of the action, offers an ongoing *carnaval* atmosphere. In the free 'Show in the Sky,' Mardi Gras floats suspended from tracks in the ceiling parade above the gaming tables while racily costumed performers dance and lip-synch to pop rock and jazzy numbers, and toss shiny beaded necklaces to the crowds. The rambunctious fun is infectious. You can even ride along in one of the floats while having your souvenir photo taken for a fee (reservations required).

Occupying most of the 'village' is an enormous casino decked out with a Brazilian motif, where 'bevertainers' bring around drinks in between doing 90-second song-and-dance numbers. In addition to 80 table games and 1200 slot machines, the Rio's poker room, home to the World Series of Poker (p133), attracts sharks. Fifty floors above the casino floor, the hokey New Orleans–themed VooDoo Lounge grants 360-degree Strip views. Lucky Strike Lanes is a mod bowling alley where hipsters and frat boys knock back Buds and watch *Monday Night Football*. After dark, illusionists Penn & Teller (p138) and the Chippendales dancers (see the boxed text, p152) entertain the good-time masses.

Cut loose, Latin-style, at the Rio

SAHARA

Standing in the no-man's-land of the North Strip, the **Sahara** (☎ 737-2111; www.saharavegas.com; 2535 Las Vegas Blvd S; Ⓜ Sahara) is a survivor. The Moroccan-themed casino is one of the few vintage Vegas icons to withstand the onslaught of corporate megaresorts. After the Sahara threw open its doors in 1952, its Conga Room showcased everyone from jazz singer Ella Fitzgerald to the Beatles.

The Moroccan theme starts at the Stripside entrance with an arched marble dome shadowed by several dozen royal palms. The *Arabian Nights* theme continues inside the casino, with gold-painted ceilings and molded columns laced with colorful vines, guarded by severe-looking statues of Middle Eastern sultans. The casino hustles the Strip's largest variety of unique card games (which will probably take all of your dough). Outside, Elvis Presley and Elizabeth Taylor once lounged by the swimming pool adorned with Moroccan mosaic tiles.

These days the Sahara is less glamorous than it sounds. Its bread-and-butter crowd is Nascar fans, who knock back bottles of Bud in the Nascar Café, ringed around Carzilla, the world's largest stock car. More compelling for speed freaks are the thrill rides, especially Speed (p83), a roller coaster that loops through the camel marquee sign.

Pretend you're back in the Fabulous '50s at the Sahara

STRATOSPHERE

Las Vegas has many buildings exceeding 20 stories, but only the **Stratosphere** (☎ 380-7777; www.stratospherehotel.com; 2000 Las Vegas Blvd S; M Sahara) tops a hundred. At 1149ft, the three-legged Stratosphere Tower is the tallest building in the USA west of the Mississippi River. At the base of the tapered tower is a casino favored by a loud-talkin', hard-drinkin' redneck crowd, but with little else in the way of a theme, although it does boast low-limit table games and 1500 reputedly loose slots and video-poker machines.

Atop the Strip's lucky landmark are viewing decks (p23), which afford spectacular 360-degree panoramas; you'll also find a revolving restaurant (p115) and a sophisticated cocktail lounge (p132). To get you there, the tower boasts the USA's fastest elevators, which lift you 108 floors in a mere 37 ear-popping seconds. Once you've recovered from the 20mph vertical rocket ride, jump on the tower's high-altitude thrill rides (p84).

Back down inside the low-roller's casino, you can buy tickets to some of the Strip's cheesiest production shows, like the laughable late-night vampire girlie show *Bite*, then spend the rest of your chump change in the nearby kingdom of kitsch, Bonanza Gifts (p98).

Brace yourselves, thrill seekers! The Stratosphere's rides are 110 stories above the Strip

TI (TREASURE ISLAND)

Yo, ho, whoa: the shift at TI (☎ 894-7111; www.treasureisland.com; 3300 Las Vegas Blvd S; 🚌 Deuce) from family-friendly to bawdy and oh-so-naughty epitomized Vegas' racy efforts to put 'sin' back in 'casino,' starting in the late '90s. Though traces of Treasure Island's original swashbuckling skull-and-crossbones theme linger (if you look hard), the reimagined TI, a terracotta-toned resort that aims to re-create an elegant Caribbean hideaway, practically screams 'leave the kids at home.'

You'll approach the property via a wood-bottomed, hemp-roped bridge that spans the artificial Sirens' Cove, set beside a vague replica of an 18th-century sea village, where the spicy *Sirens of TI* show (p81) is staged several times nightly, weather permitting. The adults-only theme continues inside the sprawling casino. One-armed Playboy bandits await where plastic chests full-o-booty once reigned. The gaming tables are tightly grouped, but no one seems to mind – the place is always packed. There's also a huge party-friendly hot tub, bikini-clad mechanical-bull-riding lasses, booze and barbecue at Gilley's (p135), and a surreal Cirque du Soleil show, *Mystère* (p146).

Easing the journey here and back is a free tram shuttling gamblers to the Mirage next door. So, now you've got a handy alibi when stopping by for a quick squeeze – of the slot-machine handles, of course.

Seek your bounty at TI (Treasure Island)

VENETIAN

Casino impresario Sheldon Adelson broke ground on his replica of La Repubblica Serenissima (Most Serene Republic) – reputed to be the home of the world's first casino – shortly after the controversial and dramatic implosion of the vintage Sands casino hotel in 1996. On this hallowed ground, the Rat Pack frolicked; this was where Frank Sinatra, Dean Martin, Sammy Davis Jr and the rest of the gang hobnobbed with movie stars, senators and showgirls during the 'Fabulous Fifties.' When the Sands tumbled down, a piece of the city's history was lost.

Inspired by the splendor of Italy's most romantic city, the luxury mega-resort **Venetian** (☎ 414-1000; www.venetian.com; 3355 Las Vegas Blvd S; Ⓜ Harrah's/Imperial Palace) boasts reproductions of Venetian landmarks including the doge's palace, *campanile* (bell tower), St Mark's Sq and even a mini Rialto Bridge with a moving walkway added. Graceful bridges, flowing canals, vibrant piazzas and stone walkways faithfully imitate the Venetian spirit, especially inside the Grand Canal Shoppes (p93), where gondolas (p84) set sail. Poker pros play high-stakes, no-limit Texas Hold'em (p175) inside the spacious casino. More mega-attractions include sultry Tao nightclub (p144); the world-class Canyon Ranch SpaClub (p148) and fitness center; and top-drawer gourmet restaurants (p116), some with star chefs confidently at the helm.

The Venetian is linked to the neighboring Palazzo casino hotel (p54) via the Shoppes at the Palazzo (p94).

Sample la dolce vita at the Venetian

WYNN & ENCORE

Instead of an exploding volcano or an Eiffel tower out front to lure the crowds, legend Steve Wynn's eponymous resort **Wynn Las Vegas** (☎ 770-7000; www.wynnlasvegas.com; 3145 Las Vegas Blvd S; 🚌 Ace Gold, Deuce) is all about exclusivity – step inside so you can snub the hoi polloi flooding Las Vegas Blvd, secure in your lavish retreat. VIPs who reserve a suite even get to use a private side entrance.

Inside the copper-toned signature resort (literally speaking, Wynn's name is written in script across the top, punctuated by a period) is awash with vibrant floral mosaics, natural light from panoramic windows and al fresco seating. Gawking tourists amble by the Ferrari/Maserati dealership's logo store (p97), haute-couture shops on the Esplanade (p95) and sumptuous restaurants (p117). Inside the enormous casino is a popular poker room attracting pros around the clock, slot machines from a penny up to $5000 per pull, and a spread of mostly high-minimum table games.

Apparently, all this still wasn't enough for Wynn, who also built next-door **Encore** (☎ 770-8000; www.encorelasvegas.com; 3111 Las Vegas Blvd S; 🚌 Ace Gold, Deuce) resort. Flash your sun-kissed skin at Encore Beach Club, or get down with the hotties at XS nightclub (p144). For nostalgic Rat Pack lovers, Sinatra restaurant (p117) is a love letter to the Chairman, while Switch steakhouse (p118) is a Vegas-worthy gimmick worth seeing once.

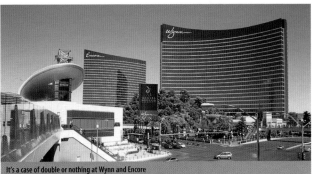

It's a case of double or nothing at Wynn and Encore

OTHER CASINOS

BALLY'S

☎ 739-4111; www.ballyslasvegas.com; 3645 Las Vegas Blvd S; Ⓜ Bally's/Paris

Unless it's 'bigger is better,' there's no real theme at the Strip's most staid megaresort, with a football-field-sized casino overhung by twinkling chandeliers and overstuffed blue-velvet chairs. But Bally's biggest attractions are not about gaming. *Jubilee!* (p145) is one of Vegas' long-running showgirl extravaganzas. After performances, the leggy dancers often pose for their over-the-hill admirers at the casino's Indigo lounge. Or visitors can peek behind the curtains on a backstage tour (p146). The monorail station is at the back, and an interior walkway connects to Paris Las Vegas.

BILL'S GAMBLIN' HALL & SALOON

☎ 737-2100; www.billslasvegas.com; 3595 Las Vegas Blvd S; Ⓜ Flamingo/Caesars Palace

Lavish Tiffany-styled stained glass, stately chandeliers and polished dark wood dominate this pint-sized neo-Victorian casino. Only downtown's Main Street Station (p67) evokes turn-of-the-20th-century Nevada better. Opened as the Barbary Coast, this 1970s-era casino claims 650 slot and video-poker machines and precious few table games. Downstairs, Drai's (p153) draws a hip post-clubbing crowd, while lounge acts like 'Big Elvis' play upstairs. Parking is almost impossible here; try walking over from the monorail line instead.

BINION'S

☎ 382-1600; www.binions.com; 128 E Fremont St; 🚌 Deuce

Opened in 1951 by notorious Texan gambler Benny Binion, who sported gold coins for buttons on his cowboy shirts, this casino became famous for its 'zero limit' betting policy, and as the place where the World Series of Poker was born. Now that Benny has gone 'all in' in the sky, the ex-Horseshoe casino is struggling to live up to its legacy. But it's worth swinging by the poker room to witness nail-biting, around-the-clock Texas Hold'em action.

BEST LOW-ROLLER DIVES

Whether you're looking for 5¢ video-poker machines or roulette wheels with 25¢ minimum bets, bravely start slumming downtown at the **Golden Gate** (opposite), **Plaza** (p67) or **El Cortez** (opposite), or on the Strip at the loud-as-hell **Casino Royale** (opposite) or the **Stratosphere** (p60).

☯ CALIFORNIA

☎ 385-1222; www.thecal.com; 12 E Ogden Ave; 🚌 Deuce

At many Vegas casinos, a lucky spin of a slot machine will earn you a brand-spanking-new BMW, a racy Jaguar or a red-hot convertible. At the downtown 'just-call-me-Cal' California, one very lucky nickel-slots player will someday ride home in – drum roll, please – a brand-new PT Cruiser! That simple fact tells you a lot about the 1970s-era Cal, 'the hotel with aloha spirit,' where even the dealers wear Hawaiian shirts, because over 80% of the Cal's guests hail from the 50th state. On the skybridge connecting to Main Street Station are photos of the Cal's Golden Arm Club, which immortalizes lucky shooters from the craps tables.

☯ CASINO ROYALE

☎ 800-854-7666; www.casinoroyale hotel.com; 3411 Las Vegas Blvd S; Ⓜ Harrah's/Imperial Palace

Tired of megaresort casinos stealing your dough courtesy of bad-odds video-poker machines and table games with ridiculous rules that inflate the house advantage (ie 'edge') beyond limits that even mobsters would find respectable? Well, the odds aren't great here either, but at least low-minimum wagers make it easier to stomach.

Cheap drinks and fast food keep die-hard low rollers sated.

☯ EL CORTEZ

☎ 385-5200; www.elcortezhotelcasino .com; 600 E Fremont St; 🚌 Deuce

A classic dive dating back to 1940, El Cortez is choked with smoke but has vintage Vegas appeal in spades. In the crowded casino, rough-edged local gamblers grudgingly allow accidental tourists like yourself to buy into the low-limit action on roulette, craps and other table games aimed at cheapskates and gambling novices. El Cortez is the kind of place where it's almost impossible to lose your shirt, but you'll need a few stiff drinks first. It's a few too many blocks east of the Fremont Street Experience.

☯ GOLDEN GATE

☎ 385-1906; www.goldengatecasino .net; 1 E Fremont St; 🚌 Deuce

This old-fashioned gambling hall and hotel has stood on the corner of Fremont and Main Sts since 1906, one year after this whistle-stop railway town was founded. The casino transformed into the Golden Gate in the 1950s, when a troupe of Italian-Americans from San Francisco decamped at what was once known as the 'Sal Sagev' (the city's name spelled backward, doncha know). Today the Golden

Gate's hypnotic mechanical sign is almost as irresistible as its famous $1.99 shrimp cocktails (p120). The snug casino boasts lively craps tables and double-deck blackjack.

HARRAH'S

☎ 369-5000; www.harrahslasvegas .com; 3475 Las Vegas Blvd S; Ⓜ Harrah's/Imperial Palace

Though it's not nearly as rambunctious as Vegas' *carnaval* casino hotel, the Rio (p58), Harrah's may be the brightest, friendliest and most playful casino on the Strip – and it's swimming with gamblers. An enormous backlit mural over the hotel's front desk depicts the greatest Las Vegas entertainers of all time, and entertainment is still the name of the game here, with the Improv comedy club (p138) and other headliner comics and magicians. After dark, try out for TJ's All-Star Karaoke (see the boxed text, p139) at the piano bar or get soused in the outdoor Carnaval Court (p134), where flair bartenders juggle fire.

IMPERIAL PALACE

☎ 731-3311; www.imperialpalace.com; 3535 Las Vegas Blvd S; Ⓜ Harrah's/ Imperial Palace

The blue-roofed pagoda facade and faux–Far East theme are hokey, but the zany atmosphere at what was once the Flamingo Capri is quite alright. The always-packed casino is decked out in bamboo and rattan under a dragon-motif ceiling. If you liked the indie movie *The Cooler*, you'll love it here. There are lots of low-minimum table games to be found here, but avoid the bad-odds blackjack in the pit. Time your visit to coincide with the evening shift change of the 'dealertainers' (p78), celebrity impersonators who do double duty as dealers, or catch the sham stars performing in *Legends in Concert* (p146) at Harrah's (see above).

Get into the spirit at Harrah's Carnaval Court (p134)

◉ MAIN STREET STATION

☎ 387-1896; www.mainstreetcasino
.com; 200 N Main St; 🚌 Deuce

Throughout the filigreed neo-Victorian casino are notable *objets d'histoire*, most keeping to the turn-of-the-20th-century theme. Look out for an art-nouveau chandelier from Paris and stained-glass windows from silent-movie star Lillian Gish's mansion. Exquisite bronze chandeliers above the casino's central pit were originally installed in the 1890s Coca-Cola Building in Austin, Texas. Ornate mahogany woodwork now gracing the hotel registration desk and players' club was lifted out of a 19th-century Kentucky drugstore. Surprisingly, a graffiti-covered chunk of the Berlin Wall now supports the urinals in the men's restroom. Self-guided tour brochures are available at the hotel lobby desk, not far from the Triple 7 brewpub (p137).

◉ MONTE CARLO

☎ 730-7777; www.montecarlo.com; 3770 Las Vegas Blvd S; 🚌 Deuce

Fronted by Corinthian colonnades, triumphal arches, petite dancing fountains and allegorical statuary, this not-so-elegant casino is still bustling and spacious. A magnificent marble-floored, crystal-chandeliered lobby with Palladian windows is reminiscent of a European grand hotel, but otherwise this is a poor person's Bellagio rather than an evocation of the grandeur of its namesake in Monaco. For entertainment, there's live music at the Pub and tacky, trashy Diablo's Cantina towering over the Strip out front.

◉ ORLEANS

☎ 365-7111; www.orleanscasino.com; 4500 W Tropicana Ave; 🚌 free Strip shuttle

A mile west of the Strip, this N'awlins-themed casino hotel has done a so-so job of re-creating the Big Easy. Among its many diversions are the 70-lane bowling alley, 18-screen cineplex and specialty bars like Brendan's Irish Pub, which has live music some nights. Entertainment legends such as Willie Nelson and LeAnn Rimes have performed in the Orleans showroom, while megaconcerts and sports events take place in the arena (see the boxed text, p151). The high-ceilinged casino is an airy, rectangular room filled with thousands of ho-hum slot machines and table games.

◉ PLAZA

☎ 386-2110; www.plazahotelcasino
.com; 1 Main St; 🚌 Deuce

Built on the site of the old Union Pacific Railroad Depot, Jackie Gaughan's Plaza is a 1970s time capsule. Like most downtown joints, the down-at-heel Plaza is made for low-rollin' gamblers. Its tacky decor doesn't correspond to any known theme, unless the theme is cheap. And that's just fine with the Plaza's patrons, who are hypnotized by the penny slots, nickel video-poker machines and $1 blackjack tables with sarcastic dealers. Feisty blue-haired ladies play for keeps upstairs in the 400-seat bingo room. Also upstairs is Firefly, a tapas bar with cockpit views of the Fremont Street Experience.

🎰 RED ROCK CASINO RESORT SPA
☎ 797-7777; www.redrocklasvegas.com; 11011 W Charleston Blvd at I-215; 🚌 206

Poised within easy striking distance of the southwestern beauty of Red Rock Canyon (p160), this slick high-concept, high-design casino resort is built for suburbanites. It banks not only on its vast casino, but also on its adventure spa (p149) and above-average restaurants, such as all-naturally delicious LBS Burger Joint (p126).

🎰 RIVIERA
☎ 734-5110; www.rivierahotel.com; 2901 Las Vegas Blvd S; 🚌 Deuce

The Riviera was the first high-rise on the Strip when it opened in 1955. Liberace did the ribbon-cutting honors. Film auteur Orson Welles appeared on stage the next year performing – of all things – magic acts. A host of big-name entertainers have starred at the Riviera ever since, including Louis Armstrong, Duke Ellington and Tony Bennett. But that Hollywood glamour has been almost entirely lost by now. Inside the dimly lit, confusingly laid-out casino, Penny and Nickel Town are faves with the old-as-the-hills clientele, who love the hot, hot slot tournies. Outside the front entrance, a bawdy bronzed statue of the Riv's showgirls is fondly fondled by drunk tourists.

🎰 SAM'S TOWN
☎ 456-7777; www.samstownlv.com; 5111 Boulder Hwy at E Flamingo Rd & S Nellis Blvd; 🚌 107, 202

It's such a landmark on the local Vegas scene, the Killers named their sophomore album after it. Ranchers, cowboys and RVers flock here, and there's a helluva lot to keep 'em all amused. It's a rip-roarin' place to get your feet wet at table games, including some single-deck blackjack and electronic roulette. Or you can just peruse the country-and-western outfitter Sheplers (p89), go bowling and take in a flick at the cinema, or feed your inner glutton at Billy

Bob's Steak House and Saloon, which dishes up a foot-long Grand Canyon chocolate layer cake.

SILVERTON
☎ 263-7777; www.silvertoncasino.com; 3333 Blue Diamond Rd, off I-15; 🚌 217
Built for the same redneck crowd as the Bass Pro Shops Outdoor World (p96) next door, here you can keep plugging nickels and quarters into all of those full-pay video-poker and slot machines, just like the RV-drivin' retirees who are camped at the RV park out back. Don't miss the coin-op miniature bowling inside an Airstream trailer at the casino's Shady Grove Lounge.

TROPICANA
☎ 739-2222; www.troplv.com; 3801 Las Vegas Blvd S; Ⓜ MGM Grand
Built in 1957, the Trop has had half a century to sully its shine, lose its crowds and go the way of the Dunes and the Sands – ashes to ashes, dust to dust. But thanks to a massive new facelift, it just keeps hanging in there. The sleek, new Miami-meets-Havana theme is a spirit-lifting change, especially in airy, light Paradise Tower rooms. Investigate the casino's mini mob museum for more vintage Vegas atmosphere. Out back, the tropically inspired pool complex has multilevel lagoon pools, streaming waterfalls and classic swim-up blackjack tables.

VEGAS CLUB
☎ 385-1664; www.vegasclubcasino.net; 18 E Fremont St; 🚌 Deuce
A sports-themed casino hotel with a Hawaiian twist, the super-friendly Vegas Club is noteworthy for its collections of sports memorabilia, such as World Series autographed baseball bats. Naturally there's a race and sports book with bleacher seats inside the low-key casino, where dealers don baseball-style uniforms just like at a real stadium. Keep an eye out for the occasional full-pay video-poker machine or double-deck blackjack table.

>LAS VEGAS

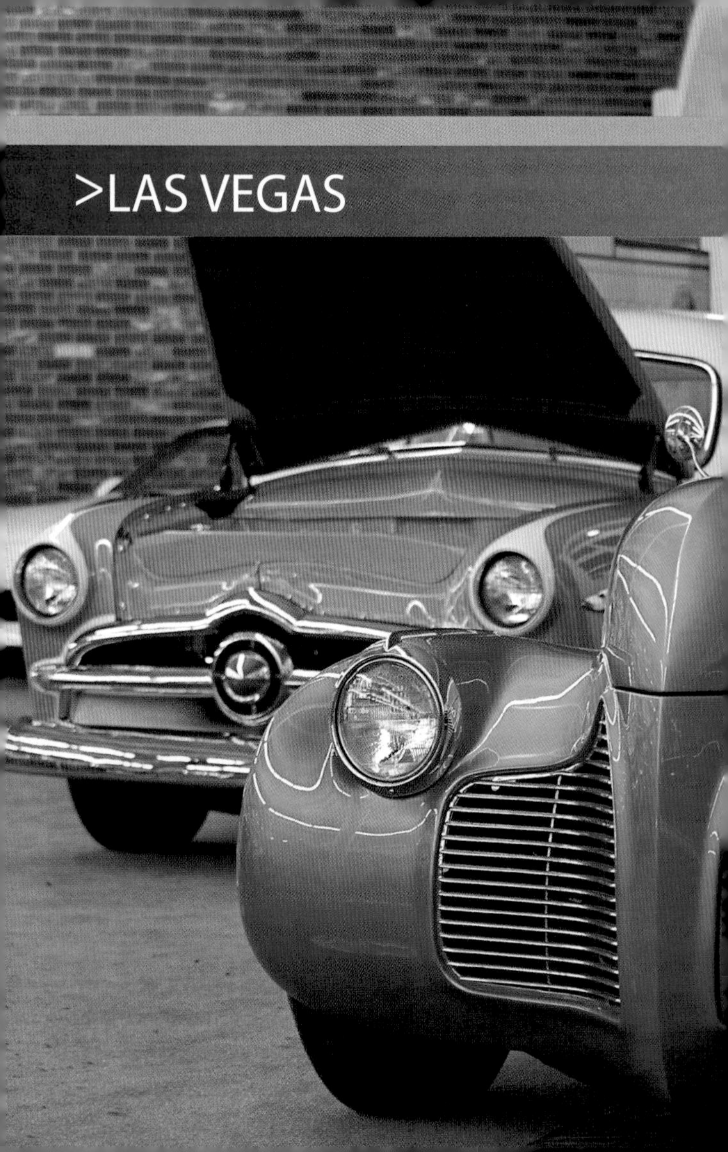

How does a classic model take your fancy? Browse the wheels at Auto Collections (p95)

👁 SEE

Baby, there's no shortage of things to see in Las Vegas. In fact, the one sure bet in this gambling-hall town is that you absolutely won't have time to see or do it all. The city itself is inexhaustible (and that's the way we like it).

That goes double for the Strip, where the vast majority of casino hotels are standing and the array of free to stratospherically priced attractions can be head-spinning. You could spend all day and night in just one of the Strip's top megaresorts, and still not experience everything it offers.

When you grow weary of all that glitz on the Strip, it's worth checking out the vintage vibe around downtown's Fremont Street Experience, the hipsters' scene in the Fremont East Entertainment and 18b Arts Districts, offbeat museums and more in Las Vegas' outlying neighborhoods, or the Southwest's desert playgrounds outside the city limits (p155).

As you ambitiously sketch out your day over a brunch buffet, remember to factor in the substantial time it takes just to get around town.

CYBER MUSEUMS

Lots of memorabilia gets cast off in this ahistorical town. Thankfully, some of it ends up in the **UNLV Special Collections** (www.library.unlv.edu/speccol), where it's closely guarded by the university. The Lied Library holds a pit boss's ransom of books, photos, maps, posters, manuscripts and more from the city's early, hurly-burly days. The best way to visit is from the comfort of your own hotel room; online exhibits are free and available 24/7/365. UNLV's **Center for Gaming Research** (http://gaming.unlv.edu/v_museum) also hosts a virtual museum with such intriguing exhibits as the photographic survey of the Strip's glorious neon, a retrospective on the World Series of Poker, Rat Pack–era memorabilia and more.

Top left Tasty treats, downtown **Bottom left** Succumb to cliché and get hitched by Elvis in a Vegas wedding chapel (p84)

ART GALLERIES & MUSEUMS

See also p79 for more unusual and outrageous museums.

ARTS FACTORY
☎ 382-3886; www.theartsfactory.com; 101-109 E Charleston Blvd; ⏱ most galleries noon-5pm Tue-Sat, to 10pm on last Fri of each month; 🚌 206

Inside you'll find hit-and-miss, but always intriguing, local artists' workshops and the Contemporary Arts Center, a community hub. Across the street, Brett Wesley Gallery (www.brettwesleygallery.com) stages contemporary photography exhibitions.

ATOMIC TESTING MUSEUM
☎ 794-5151; www.atomictesting museum.org; 755 E Flamingo Rd; adult/concession $12/9; ⏱ 10am-5pm Mon-Sat, noon-5pm Sun; 🚌 202

Explore the modern history of atomic weapons in the Southwest USA desert at this top-notch multimedia museum. View historic footage inside the Ground Zero Theater, which mimics a concrete test bunker, after buying your tickets at the replica Nevada Test Site guard station. For more background on the museum, see p15.

BELLAGIO GALLERY OF FINE ART
☎ 693-7871, 877-957-9777; www.bellagio.com; Bellagio, 3600 Las Vegas Blvd S; adult $15, concession $10-12; ⏱ 10am-6pm Sun-Tue & Thu, 10am-7pm Wed, Fri & Sat, last entry 30min before closing; Ⓜ Bally's/Paris

Since Steve Wynn sold his baby to MGM Mirage, the Bellagio hasn't been blessed with the same world-class art, but its petite fine-arts gallery still hosts blockbuster traveling shows. Original masterworks also hang inside the casino hotel's Picasso restaurant.

Get up close at the Arts Factory

 Rick Harrison
Reality-TV star & co-owner of Gold & Silver Pawn (p99)

What's the biggest misconception that people have about pawn shops?
Hollywood has vilified pawn shops. But up until the 1950s, pawn shops were
the number-one form of consumer credit in the US. **How did you get to be
a jack-of-all-trades expert?** I'm a bookworm. I used to go home and read
for literally three or four hours every night, especially history books. **How has
your TV show *Pawn Stars* on the History Channel changed your business?** Before I would buy almost every other item that customers brought
in, but now I can go all day long just wading through the weirdest, most
bizarre stuff. **What's the strangest item someone has tried to sell you?**
An original Colonel Sanders suit (from Kentucky Fried Chicken). **Ever have
buyer's remorse?** I bought $40K worth of diamonds, then the police came
and took 'em away because the stones were stolen. **Advice for first-time
Vegas visitors?** Don't play roulette.

◑ CLARK COUNTY MUSEUM

☎ 455-7955; www.accessclarkcounty
.com; 1830 S Boulder Hwy, Henderson;
adult/concession $1.50/1; ⏱ 9am-
4:30pm; ⛟ 402; ♿

On the valley outskirts, this hum-
ble but jam-packed museum
merits a stop en route to Hoover
Dam. Inside you'll find exhibits on
the history of Las Vegas as an ancient sea, Native American camp
and Western frontier town. Step
outside the museum onto Heritage
St and walk through beautifully
restored historic houses.

◑ COMMERCE STREET STUDIOS

☎ 678-6278; www.commercestreet
studios.com; 1551 S Commerce St;
⏱ hours vary; ⛟ 108

In downtown's 18b Arts District,
these eclectic and independent artists' studios are ground zero for all
of the First Friday (p14) hoopla.

◑ EROTIC HERITAGE MUSEUM

☎ 369-6442; www.eroticheritage.
org; 3275 Industrial Rd; suggested
donation $15; ⏱ 6-10pm Wed & Thu,
3pm-midnight Fri, noon-midnight Sat &
Sun; ⛟ 213

Garishly lit by purple neon next to
a strip club, this warehouse-sized
temple of porn is a strange paradise
of art, film and erotic paraphernalia.
Gawk at a gigantic penis made of
10,000 copper pennies, then head

upstairs to uncensored XXX-movie
screening rooms. Need a Sin City
souvenir? Some artwork is for sale.

◑ NEON MUSEUM

☎ 387-6366; www.neonmuseum.org;
⏱ Fremont St galleries 24hr, boneyard
tours by reservation only; ⛟ Ace Gold
(Fremont St), 113 (boneyard)

Plaques tell the story of each sign
in this alfresco assemblage of vintage neon. Genie lamps, glowing
martini glasses and 1940s motel
marquees brighten up downtown,
especially inside the Neonopolis
and on cul-de-sacs north of the
Fremont Street Experience (p80).
Tours of the giant 'boneyard' of
rescued signs are by appointment
only. The permanent museum is
still a work-in-progress.

◑ SPRINGS PRESERVE

☎ 822-7700; www.springspreserve.org;
333 S Valley View Blvd; adult $19, conces-
sion $11-17; ⏱ 10am-6pm; ⛟ 207; ♿

A major 'green' achievement for
the city, this fascinating museum
complex (also see p24) weaves
together the natural and cultural
history of Las Vegas in the Origen
Experience museum, and exam-
ines a more sustainable future in
the Desert Living Center. Walk the
desert gardens and interpretive
trails, sup at chef Wolfgang Puck's
eco-cafe and pick up wildflower
seeds in the gift shop.

⊙ UNLV MARJORIE BARRICK MUSEUM

☎ 895-3381; http://barrickmuseum.unlv.edu; 4505 S Maryland Parkway; suggested donation adult/concession $5/2; ⏱ 8am-4:45pm Mon-Fri, 10am-2pm Sat; 🚌 109; ♿

Learn about Las Vegas' original in-habitants – the southern Paiutes – and other Native American tribes from around the Southwest, along with pre-Columbian American arti-facts. Outside is a small xeriscaped garden of Mojave Desert plants. During spring and fall, the univer-sity sponsors a free science lecture series that's open to the public.

⊙ GARDENS & WILDLIFE

The trails and gardens at the eco-conscious Springs Preserve (opposite and p24) are open daily by donation.

⊙ BELLAGIO CONSERVATORY & BOTANICAL GARDEN

☎ 693-7111; www.bellagio.com; Bellagio, 3600 Las Vegas Blvd S; ⏱ 24hr; Ⓜ Bally's/Paris

Beyond the hotel lobby, itself adorned with Dale Chihuly's sculpture of 2000 vibrant hand-blown glass flowers, the Bellagio's conservatory houses ostentatious floral arrangements that are bi-zarrely installed by crane through a soaring 50ft-high ceiling. The effect is ridiculously unnatural, but that doesn't stop crowds from gathering.

⊙ FLAMINGO WILDLIFE HABITAT

☎ 733-3111; www.flamingolasvegas.com; Flamingo, 3555 Las Vegas Blvd S; ⏱ 24hr; Ⓜ Flamingo/Caesars Palace

Escape from the casino madness into a dozen acres of gardens, pools, waterfalls and waterways that are filled with swans, exotic birds and ornamental koi (carp). Chilean flamingos and African penguins wander around, and palm trees and jungle plants flourish in the midst of the desert.

⊙ LION HABITAT AT MGM GRAND

☎ 891-1111; www.mgmgrand.com; MGM Grand, 3799 Las Vegas Blvd S; ⏱ 11am-7pm; Ⓜ MGM Grand

MGM owns many of the mag-nificent felines, all descendants of the movie company's original mascot, but only two are shown off in this multimillion-dollar en-closure at any given time. The big cats sprawl atop a walk-through tunnel, separated from your head by only a sheet of protective glass and a few feet of air. The animals do look rudely confined, though.

MIRAGE CASINO HOTEL

☎ 791-7111; www.mirage.com; Mirage, 3400 Las Vegas Blvd S; ⊙ 24hr; Ⓜ Harrah's/Imperial Palace
This high-roller casino is replete with a rainforest atrium under a 100ft-tall conservatory dome filled with jungle foliage, meandering streams and soothing cascades. Woven into the waterscape are scores of bromeliads fed by a computerized misting system. Exotic scents waft through the hotel lobby, where a 20,000-gallon saltwater aquarium harbors 60 species of tropical critters, from puffer fish to pygmy sharks.

SHARK REEF

☎ 632-4555; www.sharkreef.com; Mandalay Bay, 3950 Las Vegas Blvd S; adult/concession $16/11; ⊙ 10am-8pm Sun-Thu, 10am-10pm Fri & Sat, last entry 1hr before closing; 🚌 Deuce
M-Bay's unusual walk-through aquarium is home to 2000 submarine beasties, including jellyfish, moray eels, stingrays and, yes, some sharks. Other rare and endangered toothy reptiles on display include some of the world's last remaining golden crocodiles. A staff of biologists, scuba-diver caretakers and naturalists are available to chat as you wander around. Better yet, go scuba diving yourself (from $650).

SIEGFRIED & ROY'S SECRET GARDEN & DOLPHIN HABITAT

☎ 791-7188; www.miragehabitat .com; Mirage, 3400 Las Vegas Blvd S; adult/concession $15/10; ⊙ 11am-5:30pm Mon-Fri, 10am-5:30pm Sat & Sun, 10am-7pm daily in summer, last entry 30min before closing; Ⓜ Harrah's/Imperial Palace
All of the feats of conservation bragged about on the free audio tour can't compensate for enclosures built much too small for animals such as snow leopards, black panthers and white lions and tigers, who roam the world's wildest places. The claustrophobic Atlantic bottlenose dolphin pools may also make animal lovers sick at heart.

QUIRKY LAS VEGAS

IMPERIAL PALACE DEALERTAINERS

☎ 731-3311; www.imperialpalace.com; Imperial Palace, 3535 Las Vegas Blvd S; ⊙ shows every 15-30min 11am-4am; Ⓜ Harrah's/Imperial Palace
Celebrity impersonators do double duty as 'dealertainers,' jumping up from the blackjack tables to show off their song-and-dance skills on stage. Show up for the shift change, usually happening around 8pm. Don't worry: Elvis never, ever leaves the building.

STRIPPER 101

Exotic dancers are Vegas icons. But sexy pole dancing as your new exercise routine? Marketed as 'pole dancing for housewives,' exotic-dancing classes are offered in Vegas to help bring out your inner blonde bombshell. The original experience, **Stripper 101** (☎ 260-7200; www .stripper101.com; V Theater, Miracle Mile Shops, 3663 Las Vegas Blvd S; classes from $40; ⏲ schedule varies; Ⓜ Bally's/Paris), is in a cabaret setting complete with strobe lights, cocktails and feather boas. It's popular with bachelorettes, who graduate with a certificate guaranteeing they're a 'genuine Las Vegas stripper.' No nudity is allowed, so bring comfy workout clothes and shoes, plus a pair of high heels to practice strutting your stuff in.

◉ LIBERACE MUSEUM
☎ 798-5595; www.liberace.org; 1775 E Tropicana Ave; adult/concession $15/10; ⏲ 10am–5pm Tue-Sat, noon–4pm Sun, guided tours 11am & 2pm Tue-Sat, 1pm Sun; 🚌 201

For connoisseurs of kitschy celebrity shrines, this memorial (p20) to 'Mr Showmanship' houses the most flamboyant art cars, outrageously cheesy costumes and ornate pianos you'll ever see. There's a hand-painted Pleyel, on which Chopin played; a Rolls-Royce covered in mirrored tiles; and a wardrobe exhibit full of feathered capes and million-dollar furs.

◉ MADAME TUSSAUDS LAS VEGAS
☎ 862-7800; www.madametussauds .com; outside Venetian, 3377 Las Vegas Blvd S; adult $25, concession $15-18; ⏲ 10am–9pm Sun-Thu, 10am–10pm Fri & Sat; Ⓜ Harrah's/Imperial Palace

By the Venetian's moving Rialto Bridge walkway is this unique interactive wax museum, where you can strike a pose with Michael Jackson, be judged by Simon Cowell like you're on *American Idol* or put on Playboy bunny ears and sit on Hugh Hefner's lap (be sure to touch him, because Hef's made of silicone – how apropos!).

◉ PINBALL HALL OF FAME
www.pinballmuseum.org; 1610 E Tropicana Ave; admission free, most games 25-50¢; ⏲ 11am–11pm Sun-Thu, 11am–midnight Fri & Sat; 🚌 201

Tim Arnold lets anyone play his 200-plus collection of vintage pinball, video-arcade and carnival-sideshow games, all dating from the 1950s to the '90s. Take time to read the handwritten cards, which describe the priceless collection. Profits from every quarter you drop into the slots go to charity. The Pinball Hall of Fame is east of the Strip, not far from the Liberace Museum.

◉ SLOTS A' FUN

☎ 734-0410; 2890 Las Vegas Blvd S;
🕑 24hr; 🚌 Deuce

For cheap booze and cheap thrills, it's tough to beat this low-brow dive. Grab a coupon book, give the giant slot machine a free spin and scarf down a few $2 beers and half-pound hot dogs. Then kick back, relax and enjoy the laughable lounge acts. Park at Circus Circus (p44) next door.

◉ SHOWY SPECTACULARS

On the Strip, many casinos compete to dream up the biggest, best free shows. Downtown, nothing beats the cheesy Fremont Street Experience.

◉ CIRCUS CIRCUS MIDWAY

☎ 734-0410; www.circuscircus.com;
Circus Circus, 2880 Las Vegas Blvd S;
🕑 shows every 30min 11am-midnight;
🚌 Deuce

Free circus acts – trapeze artists, high-wire workers, jugglers and unicyclists – steal center stage directly above this Austin Powers–era casino's main floor. Over in the peanut gallery, grab a free seat at the revolving Horse-A-Round Bar, made famous by Hunter S Thompson's gonzo-journalism epic *Fear and Loathing in Las Vegas*.

◉ FOUNTAINS OF BELLAGIO

☎ 693-7111; www.bellagio.com;
Bellagio, 3600 Las Vegas Blvd S;
🕑 shows every 30min 3-8pm Mon-Fri, noon-8pm Sat & Sun, every 15min 8pm-midnight daily; Ⓜ Bally's/Paris

With a backdrop of Tuscan architecture, the Bellagio's faux Lake Como and dancing fountains are the antithesis of the desert – although they do recycle and use reclaimed water. The fountain show's recorded soundtrack varies, so cross your fingers that it will be Italian opera or Ol' Blue Eyes crooning 'Luck Be a Lady,' instead of country-western twang.

◉ FREMONT STREET EXPERIENCE

☎ 678-5777; www.vegasexperience.com; Fremont St, btwn Main St & Las Vegas Blvd; 🕑 shows hourly dusk-midnight; 🚌 Ace Gold, Deuce

The 1400ft-long canopy over downtown's Fremont St is steroid-enhanced by 550,000 watts of concert-hall sound and a super-big Viva Vision screen. When the 12.5-million synchronized LEDs come on, cheesy sound-and-light shows are awesome enough to hypnotize every spectator (especially drunks). A misting system built into the canopy spritzes cool relief on steamy, hot summer days.

WELCOME TO FABULOUS LAS VEGAS

South of the Strip is the city's iconic **Welcome to Fabulous Las Vegas Nevada sign** (5200 Las Vegas Blvd S, south of W Russell Rd). Just look for all the limos and tour buses unloading camera-happy tourists, who pose for souvenir photos with Elvis impersonators next to the vintage sign.

Of course, when Betty Willis designed it in 1959 with an atomic-modern starburst at the top, it wasn't fabulously retro – it was cutting-edge hip. If you miss out on a real-live photo op, you can order a mini working model of the sign (it lights up! it flashes!) online at www.lvsignco.com.

⊙ MIRAGE VOLCANO

☎ 791-7111; www.mirage.com; Mirage, 3400 Las Vegas Blvd S; ⏱ shows hourly 8pm-midnight, starting 6pm/7pm in winter/spring; Ⓜ Harrah's/Imperial Palace

When the Mirage's trademark artificial volcano erupts out of a three-acre lagoon with a roar, it inevitably brings traffic on the Strip to a screeching halt. Be on the lookout for wisps of smoke escaping from the top that signal the fiery Polynesian-style inferno is about to begin.

⊙ SIRENS OF TI

☎ 894-7111; www.treasureisland.com; TI (Treasure Island), 3300 Las Vegas Blvd S; ⏱ shows 7pm, 8:30pm & 10pm (also 5:30pm winter & 11:30pm summer), weather permitting; ⛟ Ace Gold, Deuce

The laughably spicy *Sirens of TI* show is a hilarious mock sea battle of the sexes that pits sultry femme-fatale pirates dressed like lingerie models against manly renegade freebooters. With a booming soundtrack and pyrotechnics, the show's ships – a Spanish privateer vessel and a British frigate – face off in the cove outside the casino.

⊙ THRILL RIDES & AMUSEMENTS

⊙ ADVENTUREDOME

☎ 794-3939; www.adventuredome. com; Circus Circus, 2880 Las Vegas Blvd S; per ride $4-7, day pass adult/concession $25/15; ⏱ 10am-midnight in summer, off-season hours vary; ⛟ Deuce

Enclosed by over 8000 pink-glass panes, Circus Circus' indoor amusement park is packed with thrills. Must-rides include the double-loop, double-corkscrew Canyon Blaster and the Sling Shot tower ride that packs a whopping four Gs of acceleration. Older kids get a rock-climbing wall, bungee-jumping area, mini golf and 4D special-effect 'ridefilms.' Clowns perform free shows throughout the day.

🕒 CONEY ISLAND EMPORIUM & ROLLER COASTER

☎ 740-6969; www.nynyhotelcasino.com; New York–New York, 3790 Las Vegas Blvd S; roller coaster $14 (day pass $25), games from 50¢; 🕙 11am-11pm Sun-Thu, 10:30am-midnight Fri & Sat, weather permitting; Ⓜ MGM Grand

Though your head and shoulders will take a beating, the coaster's heartline twist-and-dive maneuver produces a sensation similar to that felt by a pilot during a barrel roll in a fighter plane. The rest of the four-minute ride includes stomach-dropping dipsy-dos, high-banked turns, a 540-degree spiral and blink-and-you'll-miss-it Strip views. Enter through the Coney Island Emporium video-game arcade (with bumper cars!).

🕒 EIFFEL TOWER EXPERIENCE

☎ 888-727-4758; www.parislasvegas.com; Paris Las Vegas, 3655 Las Vegas Blvd S; adult/concession $10/7, after 7:15pm $15; 🕙 9:30am-12:30am, weather permitting; Ⓜ Bally's/Paris

How authentic is the half-scale tower? Gustave Eiffel's original drawings were consulted, but the 46-story ersatz replica is welded rather than riveted together. It's also fireproof and engineered to withstand a major earthquake. Ascend in a glass elevator to the observation deck for panoramic

No French required at the Eiffel Tower Experience

views over the Strip, the Las Vegas Valley and the rugged desert mountains.

🕒 GAMEWORKS

☎ 432-4263; www.wegotfamily.com; Showcase Mall, 3785 Las Vegas Blvd S; games 50¢-$3.50, 1hr/2hr/3hr/all-day unlimited play $20/25/30/35; 🕙 10am-midnight Sun-Thu, 10am-1am Fri & Sat; Ⓜ MGM Grand

Conceived by Steven Spielberg and developed by DreamWorks SKG with Sega and Universal Studios, this high-tech arcade inhabits a large underground space with a full bar, pool tables, loads of multiplayer virtual-reality games (bring lots of buddies) and classic joystick joys like Asteroids. It's mostly crowded with kids during the day – show up late-night for an over-18 scene.

POLE POSITION RACEWAY

☎ 227-7223; www.polepositionraceway.com; 4175 S Arville St; races per adult/junior $25/22; ⏰ 11am-11pm Sun-Thu, 11am-midnight Fri & Sat; 🚌 202

Dreamed up by Nascar and Supercross racing champs, this European-style raceway modeled on Formula One road courses boasts the fastest indoor go-karts in the USA, exciting whether you're a teen novice or a full-grown adult speed freak. Drivers must be 48in/56in tall to join the junior/adult kart races.

RICHARD PETTY DRIVING EXPERIENCE

☎ 800-237-3889; www.drivepetty.com; Las Vegas Motor Speedway, 7000 Las Vegas Blvd N, off I-15; ⏰ schedule varies

Curious about what it's like to be in high-speed pursuit? Here's your chance to ride shotgun during a Nascar-style qualifying run ($159) or drive yourself ($399) in a 600-horsepower stock car reaching speeds of over 150mph. Also at the Speedway (p151),

the **Mario Andretti Racing Experience** (☎ 877-722-3527; www.andrettiracing.com) offers cheaper ride-along and race opportunities.

SKYJUMP

☎ 800-998-6937; www.skyjumplasvegas.com; Stratosphere, 2000 Las Vegas Blvd S; jumps $100; ⏰ 11am-1am Sun-Thu, 11am-2am Fri & Sat, weather permitting; Ⓜ Sahara

The most bad-ass of the Stratosphere Tower's thrill rides (see p84), this 855ft controlled free fall drops you at speeds up to 40mph. Your entourage can even watch you fall from the tower's 108th-floor observation deck.

SPEED & CYBER SPEEDWAY

☎ 737-2111; www.saharavegas.com; Sahara, 2535 Las Vegas Blvd S; single ride/all-day pass $10/23; ⏰ Speed noon-8pm Mon-Thu, noon-10pm Fri-Sun, Cyber Speedway noon-10pm daily; Ⓜ Sahara

The Speedway's Indy car simulators are so lifelike that they excite real Formula One drivers. The artificial racers are bolted to hydraulic platforms fronting wraparound screens that are adrenaline-pumping in their realism. Speed, an electromagnetic roller coaster, slingshots to a top speed of 70mph as it zooms through the Sahara's signature marquee.

☾ STRATOSPHERE TOWER

☎ 380-7777; www.stratospherehotel
.com; Stratosphere, 2000 Las Vegas Blvd
S; elevator adult/concession $16/10,
incl 3 thrill rides $30, all-day pass $36;
⌚ 10am-1am Sun-Thu, 10am-2am Fri &
Sat, weather permitting; Ⓜ Sahara
The world's highest thrill rides
await, a whopping 110 stories
above the Strip. Big Shot straps
riders into completely exposed
seats that zip up the tower's pinnacle, while Insanity spins riders
out over the tower's edge. Views
from xScream are good, but the
ride itself is a dud. If you want an
adrenaline rush, save your dough
for the SkyJump (p83) instead.

☾ VENETIAN GONDOLAS

☎ 414-4300; www.venetian.com;
Venetian, 3355 Las Vegas Blvd S; per
person $16, private 2-passenger ride
$64; ⌚ 10am-10:45pm Sun-Thu,
10am-11:45pm Fri & Sat, outdoor noon-
10:45pm daily, reduced hours Oct-Apr;
Ⓜ Harrah's/Imperial Palace
Graceful bridges, flowing canals,
vibrant piazzas and stone walkways almost capture the romantic
spirit of Venice inside the Grand
Canal Shoppes (p93), especially
when viewed from the seat of a
floating gondola. Rides are short
(under 15 minutes), but sweet.
Same-day, in-person reservations
required.

☾ WEDDING CHAPELS

Before you get hitched, you'll need
a marriage license (see p168).

☾ A SPECIAL MEMORY WEDDING CHAPEL

☎ 384-2211, 800-962-7798; www
.aspecialmemory.com; 800 S 4th St;
⌚ 8am-10pm Sun-Thu, 8am-midnight
Fri & Sat; 🚌 Deuce
The drive-up window on Lovers
Lane has a wedding menu board
(limo-ride packages cost from
$199, and don't forget to tip the
minister). Wedding cake, photos
and videography, or an appearance by Elvis or Cher are priced à
la carte.

☾ GRACELAND WEDDING CHAPEL

☎ 382-0091, 800-824-5732; www
.gracelandchapel.com; 619 Las Vegas
Blvd S; ⌚ 9am-11pm; 🚌 Ace Gold
Offering the original Elvis impersonator wedding (from $199) for
over 50 years. If it's good enough
for rock stars, then it's probably
good enough for you, too.

☾ LITTLE CHURCH OF THE WEST

☎ 739-7971, 800-821-2452; www
.littlechurchlv.com; 4617 Las Vegas Blvd S;
⌚ 8am-midnight; 🚌 Deuce
Beginners' wedding packages cost
just $199 at this quiet, quaint little

wooden chapel built in 1942, in the shadow of the South Strip, as seen in the classic Elvis movie *Viva Las Vegas*. Spanish- and French-speaking ministers are available (by reservation only).

◎ MAVERICK HELICOPTERS
☎ 261-0007, 888-261-4414; www.maverickhelicopter.com; ⏱ by reservation only
Take a flight with Grand Canyon (p156) or Valley of Fire (p158) wedding packages (from $3529), including videography, flowers for the bride and groom, a champagne toast and wedding cake upon landing. Up to three guests fly free.

◎ VEGAS WEDDING CHAPEL
☎ 933-3464, 800-823-4095; www.702wedding.com; 555 S 3rd St; ⏱ 9am-midnight; 🚌 105, Ace Gold
Here you've got the only walk-up wedding window in the world, plus a cathedral-esque chapel, sunset terrace and gardens.

Weddings can also be arranged at scenic outdoor spots in the desert and mountains, as well as at the Grand Canyon.

◎ VIVA LAS VEGAS WEDDINGS
☎ 384-0771, 800-574-4450; www.viva lasvegasweddings.com; 1205 Las Vegas Blvd S; ⏱ office 9am-5pm, ceremony reservations 11am-9pm; 🚌 Deuce
Wacky themed wedding ceremonies (imagine vampires, Harley hogs or Cirque du Soleil–esque aerial acrobats), which can be broadcast online, are as kitschy as all get-out. More traditional wedding packages cost from $199.

◎ WEE KIRK O' THE HEATHER
☎ 382-9830, 800-843-5266; www.weekirk.com; 231 Las Vegas Blvd S; ⏱ 10am-8pm; 🚌 Deuce
The oldest continuously operating wedding chapel in Las Vegas (since 1940), and it's conveniently close to the county marriage bureau. Wedding packages booked online cost from just $90.

🛍 SHOP

Surprisingly, Las Vegas has evolved into a sophisticated shopping destination. International haute-couture purveyors on the Strip cater to cashed-up clientele, whether it's catwalk fashions fresh off this year's runways, diamond jewels once worn by royalty or imported sports cars. But Sin City is still the kind of place where porn-star-worthy bling, Elvis wigs and other tacky trash just flies off the shelves, too.

If all you want is a T-shirt, bumper sticker or shot glass announcing that you've finally been to 'Fabulous Las Vegas,' tacky souvenirs are everywhere. But if you're looking for something more unusual, the city's specialty shops are full of cool kitsch and priceless collectibles, from vintage casino memorabilia to showgirls' feather boas and real-life poker tables.

Retail shopping hours are normally 10am to 9pm (to 6pm Sunday), but casino shops, arcades and malls typically stay open until 11pm (midnight on Friday and Saturday). Christmas is one of the few holidays when most shops close.

SHOPPING AREAS

Megamalls dominate the scene. The Strip has the highest-octane shopping action, with upscale boutiques found inside casino resorts from Encore south to Mandalay Place. Downtown and west of the Strip are where to cruise for wigs, naughty adult goods and trashy lingerie. Vintage clothing stores, antiques shops and art galleries are reviving downtown's 18b Arts District, radiating outward from the intersection of Main St and Charleston Blvd. East of the Strip near UNLV, Maryland Parkway is chock-a-block with hip, cheapo shops. Trendy one-off boutiques are scarce, but they're popping up in the 'burbs, where discount outlet malls are found.

Top left The Crystals mall at CityCenter (p92) is sure to impress **Bottom left** Glam it up at Rainbow Feather Dyeing Co (p99)

CLOTHING & JEWELRY

THE ATTIC

☎ 388-4088; http://atticvintage.com; 1018 S Main St; ☿ 10am-6pm Tue-Sat; 🚍 Ace Gold

At this fantastic vintage emporium, easily spotted by its pink zebra-striped exterior, be mesmerized by fabulous hats, outrageous wigs, hippie-chic clubwear and lounge-lizard furnishings. Bling-bling costume jewelry, zany shoes and disco-inferno and glam-rock outfits are part of the way-out-there collections. Be prepared for the sky-high prices, attitudinous staff and oddball customers.

BUFFALO EXCHANGE

☎ 791-3960; www.buffaloexchange .com; 4110 S Maryland Parkway; ☿ 10am-8pm Mon-Sat, 11am-7pm Sun; 🚍 109, 202

Trade in your nearly new garb for cash or credit at this savvy secondhand chain. Don't worry: it has combed through the dingy thrift-store stuff and culled only the best 1940s to '80s vintage, clubwear, costuming goodies and designer duds.

Get the vintage vibe at The Attic

LAS VEGAS

SHOP

☐ FRED LEIGHTON
☎ 693-7050; www.fredleighton.com;
Via Bellagio, 3600 Las Vegas Blvd S;
🕙 10am-midnight; Ⓜ Bally's/Paris
Many of Hollywood's red-carpet
adornments are on loan from the
world's most prestigious collection of antique jewelry, notably
art deco and art nouveau. In Las
Vegas, unlike at the uptight NYC
outlet, they'll let almost anyone try
on finery that once belonged to
royalty. Price tags for pieces easily
top $1 million at this veritable
museum of jewels.

☐ FRUITION
☎ 796-4139; http://fruitionlv.com; 4139
S Maryland Parkway; 🕙 11am-7pm
Mon-Sat; 🚌 109, 202
Love hard-to-find pop styles from
the 1980s and '90s? Or vintage
treasures from designers like Fendi
or Ralph Lauren? This shop is a
touchable fashion archive, with
heart-attack prices to match.

☐ SHEPLERS
☎ 454-5266; www.sheplers.com; Sam's
Town, 5111 Boulder Hwy; 🕙 10am-
10pm; 🚌 107, 202
In business since 1899, this reliable
Western outfitter has everything
you'll need to dress up like a real
cowboy or cowgirl: blue jeans,
button-down shirts, leather
jackets, felt fur hats and even em-
broidered ostrich-skin boots.

☐ SUITE 160
☎ 304-2513; www.suite160.com;
Mandalay Place, 3930 Las Vegas Blvd S;
🕙 10am-11pm Sun-Thu, 10am-
midnight Fri & Sat; 🚌 Deuce
This sneaker boutique stays under
the radar, but still carries the hip-
pest kicks in ubercool collectible
styles for outfitting urban legends
in the making. Check the website
for new releases, like anniversary
Air Jordans or hemp Gazelles by
Adidas, then get here ASAP (as
they say, 'Don't sleep!').

☐ VALENTINO'S ZOOTSUIT CONNECTION
☎ 383-9555; www.valentinoszootsuit
connection.com; 107 E Charleston Blvd;
🕙 11am-5pm Mon-Sat; 🚌 Ace Gold
Lots of timeless outfits get cast off
in this ahistorical town. Some end
up at this upscale resale boutique,
which specializes in men's and
women's clothing from the turn
of the 20th century right through
to the 1970s. A sweet (and stylish!)
husband-and-wife team outfits
party-goers with custom swinging
zootsuits, cocktail dresses, Old Hollywood glamour gowns, fringed
Western wear and felt fedoras.

☐ WILLIAMS COSTUME CO
☎ 384-1384; 1226 S 3rd St; 🕙 10am-
5:15pm Mon-Sat; 🚌 Ace Gold
Williams Costume Company has
supplied the Strip's starlets with

do-it-yourself costuming goods since 1957. Check out the headshots in the dressing rooms, then go pick up some rhinestones, sequins, feathers etc – you go, girl. Costume rentals are also available.

MUSIC & BOOKS

For riveting reads about Las Vegas, see p185.

ASSOULINE
☎ 795-0166; www.assouline.com; Crystals, 3720 Las Vegas Blvd S; ✆ 10am-midnight; 🚌 Deuce

High-concept, design-savvy art, architecture, photography and fashion books abound, many published in exquisitely illustrated editions. Beautifully preserved rare and vintage titles are specialties, including gambling and Las Vegas pop histories. Gift wrapping reflects the shop's motto: books are works of art.

BAUMAN RARE BOOKS
☎ 948-1617; www.baumanrarebooks .com; Shoppes at the Palazzo, 3327 Las Vegas Blvd S; ✆ 10am-11pm; Ⓜ Harrah's/Imperial Palace

Hidden inside the Palazzo, enter a bibliophile's paradise, where rare and first editions of the *Wizard of Oz* and Truman Capote's *In Cold Blood* stand on giant-sized shelves. Lavishly illustrated antiquarian

titles lie under glass display cases. Staff may raise their eyebrows at casual browsers, who may *not* touch the tomes.

GAMBLERS BOOK SHOP
☎ 382-7555, 800-522-1777; www .gamblersbook.com; 5473 S Eastern Ave; ✆ 9am-5pm Mon-Fri; 🚌 110

This off-the-beaten-path gem stocks just about every book ever written about gaming strategy and Las Vegas, including out-of-print titles. The clientele, some of whom look as if they might have been around since the Rat Pack era, can dispense valuable edge-beating advice.

ZIA RECORDS
☎ 735-4942; www.ziarecords.com; 4225 S Eastern Ave; ✆ 10am-midnight; 🚌 110, 202

Calling itself the 'last real record store,' this Arizona-based vendor has a warehouse full of ear-tickling sounds, including a locals-only section where you just might dig up a demo by the next breakout Vegas band. Live in-store performances happen on a stage with the warning sign: 'No slam dancing.'

NAUGHTY NOVELTIES

There are full-service lingerie shops inside many strip clubs (p150). All those hard-working beefy guys and sultry women obviously don't have time to make their own G-strings and tasseled undies!

ADULT SUPERSTORE

☎ 798-0144; www.adultss.net; 3850 W Tropicana Ave; ☽ 24hr; ☒ 201
This enormous, well-lit porn warehouse is a sexual fantasyland of toys, books, porn magazines and movies, 'marital enhancement products' and titillating accessories. Solo guys gravitate toward the XXX arcade upstairs.

BARE ESSENTIALS

☎ 247-4711; www.bareessentialsvegas .com; 4029 W Sahara Ave; ☽ 10am-7pm Mon-Sat, noon-5pm Sun; ☒ 204
Pros swear by BE for business attire. It's heavy on theme wear – lots of cheerleader and schoolgirl outfits. Next door, **Bad Attitude Boutique** (☎ 646-9669; www.badattitude. com; ☽ 11am-7pm Mon-Fri, noon-7pm Sat, noon-5pm Sun) makes custom-made corsets and bustiers, goth fetish wear and burlesque fashions, while neighboring **Red Shoes** (☎ 889-4442; ☽ 10:30am-8pm Mon-Sat, noon-6:30pm Sun) stocks knee-high boots, stripper stilettos and glittery platforms.

DÉJÀ VU LOVE BOUTIQUE

☎ 731-5655; 3247 Industrial Rd; ☽ 24hr; ☒ 213
Sidling up next to a strip club, this candy-colored sex shop stays open around the clock. Drop in for a

> ### UNIQUE BOUTIQUES
> > Annie Creamcheese (Shoppes at the Palazzo; p94)
> > Bettie Page (Miracle Mile Shops; p94)
> > Fruition (p89)
> > Kiki de Montparnasse (Crystals; below)
> > Stash (Miracle Mile Shops; p94)

pick-me-up, maybe passionfruit-flavored lube, a bouncy paddle or a very adult DVD to enjoy in your hotel room. Bachelor/bachelorette parties welcome.

KIKI DE MONTPARNASSE

☎ 736-7883; www.kikidm.com; Crystals, 3720 Las Vegas Blvd S; ☽ 10am-midnight; ☒ Deuce
Let the 'romance concierge' lead you through this high-end boudoir boutique spilling over with classy lingerie, towering heels and 'instruments of pleasure.' The couples' dressing room even has a portrait booth.

PARADISE ELECTRO STIMULATIONS

☎ 474-2991, 800-339-6953; www.pes electro.com; 1509 W Oakey Blvd; ☽ 10am-6pm Mon-Fri, noon-6pm Sat; ☒ 409
'Innovating human sexuality since 1986,' this dungeon-esque fetish

boutique is tucked away on the wrong side of the tracks. It's the exotic, neon-lit home of owner Dante Amore's legendary auto-erotic chair, which must be seen (and felt) to be believed. Yeeowch.

🏠 STRINGS BOUTIQUE
☎ 873-7820; 4970 Arville St; www.stringsvegas.com; ☽ noon-7:30pm Mon-Sat; 🚌 104, 201

It's no surprise to see a Hummer limo parked outside this industrial strip-mall warehouse of adult and fetish fashions. Watch go-go and exotic dancers get dressed (or un-dressed, rather) from head to toe here, with jewelry, platform shoes and the shortest skirts and scanti-est G-strings you've ever seen. Custom-made designs available.

🏬 SHOPPING MALLS & ARCADES

🏠 CRYSTALS
☎ 590-9299; www.crystalsatcitycenter.com; CityCenter, 3720 Las Vegas Blvd S; ☽ 10am-midnight; 🚌 Deuce

Its metal-and-glass facade look-ing like an angular Frank Gehry design, this mall wins on looks alone. Inside you'll find decadent designer boutiques (Louis Vuitton, Versace, Nanette Lepore, Carolina Herrera and Roberto Cavalli), exquisite jewelers and specialty shops Assouline (p90) and Kiki de Montparnasse (p91).

🏠 THE DISTRICT
☎ 564-8595, 877-564-8595; www.thedistrictatgvr.com; Green Valley Ranch, 2240 Village Walk Dr, Henderson, off I-215 exit Green Valley Parkway; ☽ 10am-9pm Mon-Sat, 11am-7pm Sun; 🚌 111

An off-Strip shopping magnet, the open-air upmarket District has a mix of chain and boutique shops and eateries, including REI, an outdoor-sports retailer; Oya Eco Couture for 'green' fashion trends; Whole Foods grocery store; and Settebello Pizzeria Napoletana.

🏠 FASHION SHOW
☎ 784-7000; www.thefashionshow.com; 3200 Las Vegas Blvd S; ☽ 10am-9pm Mon-Sat, 11am-7pm Sun; 🚌 Ace Gold

Size *does* matter. Though unique shops are sparse at Nevada's biggest and flashiest mall, there are 250-plus chain storefronts, all anchored by giant department stores, plus popular eateries inside and out (p106). It's all topped off by 'The Cloud,' a multimedia canopy that resembles a flamenco hat.

🏠 FORUM SHOPS
☎ 893-6189; www.simon.com; Caesars Palace, 3500 Las Vegas Blvd S; ☽ 10am-11pm Sun-Thu, 10am-midnight Fri & Sat; Ⓜ Flamingo/Caesars Palace

Franklins fly out of Fendi bags faster here than in the high-roller casinos. Caesars' fanciful homage to an ancient Roman marketplace houses 160 designer emporia, including one-name catwalk wonders such as Armani and Versace; specialty boutiques like fashionable Intermix and Agent Provocateur for lingerie; Kiehl's old-world apothecary and modern MAC cosmetics; and Max Brenner's haute designer chocolates.

 GRAND CANAL SHOPPES

☎ 414-4500; www.thegrandcanal shoppes.com; Venetian, 3377 Las Vegas Blvd S; ☷ 10am-11pm Sun-Thu, 10am-midnight Fri & Sat; Ⓜ Harrah's/Imperial Palace

Wandering minstrels, jugglers and laughable living statues perform at St Mark's Sq inside this Italianate mall. Cobblestone walkways wind past bebe, Godiva, Kenneth Cole, Movado, Sephora and 80 other luxury shops. The doors are thrown open for early-bird window shopping at 7am. Don't want to walk? Take a leisurely gondola ride (p84).

 HARD ROCK

☎ 693-5000; www.hardrockhotel.com; Hard Rock, 4455 Paradise Rd; ☷ most shops 10am-11pm Sun-Thu, 10am-midnight Fri & Sat; ▣ 108

For pop-star clothing brands and rare rock 'n' roll collectibles, hit this casino's logo shop and rockin' John Varvatos and Affliction boutiques.

Peruse Rocks, a 24-hour jewelry store, after winning big at the poker tables. Love Jones tempts with devilish lingerie and sex toys.

 MANDALAY PLACE

☎ 632-7777; www.mandalaybay.com; btwn Mandalay Bay & Luxor, 3930 Las Vegas Blvd S; ☷ 10am-11pm Sun-Thu, 10am-midnight Fri & Sat; ▣ Deuce

With a de-stress atmosphere and vaulted ceilings, M-Bay's airy promenade shows off almost two

Retail therapy awaits at the Fashion Show mall

dozen unique boutiques, including Suite 160 (p89), Metropark and Urban Outfitters for tweens, Lush beauty shop (p98), the Art of Shaving and ARCS salon, and the first-ever Nike Golf store.

☐ MIRACLE MILE SHOPS
☎ 866-0703; www.miraclemile shopslv.com; Planet Hollywood, 3663 Las Vegas Blvd S; ☼ 10am-11pm Sun-Thu, 10am-midnight Fri & Sat; Ⓜ Bally's/Paris

Measuring an incredible 1.5 miles long, this sleekly redesigned mall harbors 170 retailers and 15 restaurants. The focus is contemporary chains, especially urban apparel. Stand-out shops include Bettie Page for mid-20th-century vintage and pin-up styles, imports H&M and Ben Sherman, the LA denim king True Religion, and Stash, Vegas' own rock-star boutique.

☐ SHOPPES AT THE PALAZZO
☎ 414-4525; www.theshoppesatthe palazzo.com; Palazzo, 3327 Las Vegas Blvd S; ☼ 10am-11pm Sun-Thu, 10am-midnight Fri & Sat; Ⓜ Harrah's/Imperial Palace

Towered over by three-story Barneys New York department store, this casino mall is a glittering galaxy of fashion stars such as Diane von Furstenberg and Cole Haan; London trendsetters Chloé and Thomas Pink; Canali for tailor-made Italian apparel; Annie Creamcheese for glam 20th-century mod fashions; Anya Hindmarch for handbags and accessories; and Jimmy Choo for divine shoes.

☐ TOWN SQUARE
☎ 269-5000; www.townsquarelas vegas.com; 6605 Las Vegas Blvd S; ☼ 10am-9:30pm Mon-Thu, 10am-10pm Fri & Sat, 11am-8pm Sun; ☐ Ace Gold

Within sight of McCarran International Airport, this polished outdoor mall lined with faux facades harbors sought-after chains such as Juicy Couture, Sephora, Apple, Abercrombie & Fitch and Metropark. Palm trees wave over pedestrian-only streets, while happy-hour bars and a state-of-the-art cinema draw in the crowds.

☐ VIA BELLAGIO
☎ 693-7111; www.bellagio.com; Bellagio, 3600 Las Vegas Blvd S; ☼ 10am-midnight; Ⓜ Bally's/Paris

Bellagio's swish indoor promenade is home to the who's who of fashion-plate designers: Prada, Armani, Gucci, Bottega Veneta, Chanel, Dior, Tiffany & Co and Fred Leighton (p89). Bring a pocket pooch and your darkest celebrity-in-disguise sunglasses.

WYNN ESPLANADE

☎ 770-7000; www.wynnlasvegas.com;
Wynn, 3131 Las Vegas Blvd S; ⏱ 10am-
11pm Sun-Thu, 10am-midnight Fri & Sat;
🚌 Ace Gold

Steve Wynn's eponymous
resort showcases 75,000 sq ft of
consumer bliss, with top-of-the-
line retailers such as Alexander
McQueen, Cartier, Chanel, Dior,
Louis Vuitton, Manolo Blahnik
and Oscar de la Renta. After you
hit the jackpot, take a test drive
at the Penske Wynn Ferrari/Maserati
dealership.

 SPECIALIST STORES

Technorati gravitate toward the
Apple Store (☎ 650-9550; www.apple.com;
⏱ 10am-9pm Mon-Sat, 11am-7pm Sun) at

the Fashion Show (p92) and **Sony
Style** (☎ 697-5420; www.sonystyle.com;
⏱ 10am-11pm Sun-Thu, 10am-midnight Fri
& Sat) at the Forum Shops (p92).

AUTO COLLECTIONS

☎ 794-3174; www.autocollections
.com; 5th fl, Imperial Palace, 3535 Las
Vegas Blvd S; adult/concession $9/5,
free coupon on website; ⏱ 10am-6pm;
Ⓜ Harrah's/Imperial Palace

Car buffs could easily pass away
hours drooling over one of the
world's largest privately owned
auto collections. Among the prized
vehicles on hand here (some
for sale) are more Bentleys and
Dusenbergs than you could toss a
chauffeur at, not to mention classic
hot rods, muscle models, Indy 500
race cars and exotic imports.

LOW-ROLLER DEALS

Brand-name bargain hunters can save a lotta moolah at these jam-packed outlet malls:
Fashion Outlets Las Vegas (☎ 874-1400, 888-424-6898; www.fashionoutletlasvegas
.com; 32100 Las Vegas Blvd S, off I-15 exit 1, Primm; ⏱ 10am-8pm) At the Nevada/
California state line, about a 40-minute drive southwest of Las Vegas, discover a mix of
more than 100 high-end (Burberry, Coach, Juicy, Michael Kors, Neiman Marcus Last Call)
and everyday (Banana Republic, J Crew, Levi's) brands. It's accessible from the Strip via a
shoppers' shuttle (round trip $15), but it's only worth the trip for Californians who already
happen to be driving by.
Las Vegas Premium Outlets (☎ 474-7500; www.premiumoutlets.com; 875 S Grand
Central Parkway; ⏱ 10am-9pm Mon-Sat, 10am-8pm Sun; 🚌 Ace Gold) The most upscale
of Vegas' outlet malls features high-end names like Armani Exchange, Calvin Klein, DKNY,
Dolce & Gabbana and Kenneth Cole, along with a few casual brands like True Religion. RTC's
Ace Gold and C-Line buses stop at the mall frequently between 7am and 10pm.

☐ BASS PRO SHOPS OUTDOOR WORLD

☎ 730-5200; www.basspro.com; 8200 Dean Martin Dr; ⏱ 9am-9pm Mon-Sat, 10am-6pm Sun; 🚌 217

Keep an eye on the handcrafted wildlife chandeliers at this redneck superstore adjacent to the Silverton casino resort. Paradise for fishers and hunters, Bass Pro stakes its claim on a ginormous showroom with a rock-climbing wall, an indoor archery range, a 40,000-gallon aquarium and a meandering stream stocked with native Nevada species.

☐ CASA FUENTE

☎ 731-5051; Forum Shops at Caesars Palace, 3500 Las Vegas Blvd S; ⏱ 10am-11pm Sun-Thu, 10am-midnight Fri & Sat; Ⓜ Flamingo/Caesars Palace

A million-dollar cigar shop with a bar that feels like a little slice of Havana: the walk-in humidor contains signature stogies from Latin America and the Caribbean (not Cuba, though – damn those US customs regulations!). Order a tropical cocktail from the petite bar, then grab a wicker chair out front.

Unearth some treasures at the Gypsy Caravan Antique Village

📷 DESERT ROCK SPORTS

☎ 254-1143; www.desertrocksportslv
.com; 8221 W Charleston Blvd, west of
S Buffalo Dr; ⏰ 9am-7pm Mon-Sat, 10am-
6pm Sun Oct-Mar, call for hours Apr-Sep;
🚌 206
Run by climbers, this outdoor-
adventure shop rents bouldering
crash pads and carries all-weather
apparel and brand-name hiking,
rock-climbing, camping and back-
packing equipment. The indoor
Red Rock Climbing Center (☎ 254-5604;
www.redrockclimbingcenter.com; 8201 W
Charleston Blvd) is next door.

📷 DOUBLE HELIX

☎ 735-9463; www.doublehelixwine.
com; Palazzo, 3327 Las Vegas Blvd S;
⏰ 10am-11pm Sun-Thu, 10am-midnight
Fri & Sat; Ⓜ Harrah's/Imperial Palace
At this wine boutique, exclusive
bottles are stacked higher than
poker chips on a WSOP final table.
Knowledgeable staff escort oenophiles through the VIP room and
proffer champagne flights outside
at the tasting bar, which dispenses
rare vintages by the glass.

📷 FERRARI STORE

☎ 770-2000; www.penskewynn
ferrari.com; Wynn Esplanade, 3131 Las
Vegas Blvd S; showroom admission $10;
⏰ 9am-8pm; 🚌 Ace Gold
Even if you can't afford to drive
one of the high-end luxury Italian
sportscars right off the casino's
dealership floor, you can still
aspire to lifestyles of the rich and
famous at the logo brand shop
next door, selling everything from
signature keychains and men's co-
logne to high-end leather jackets.

📷 FIELD OF DREAMS

☎ 792-8233; www.fieldofdreams.com;
Forum Shops at Caesars Palace, 3500 Las
Vegas Blvd S; ⏰ 10am-11pm Sun-Thu,
10am-midnight Fri & Sat; Ⓜ Flamingo/
Caesars Palace
The first name in sports and
celebrity memorabilia in Las
Vegas, Field of Dreams deserves a
look whether you are interested
in buying or not. Among the
items that have been sold here
is a baseball autographed and
inscribed with an apology by dis-
graced baseball legend Pete Rose,
who sometimes makes in-store
appearances.

📷 GYPSY CARAVAN ANTIQUE
VILLAGE

☎ 868-3302; 1302 S 3rd St; ⏰ 10am-
5pm Tue-Sat; 🚌 Ace Gold
One person's trash truly is another
person's treasure, as the saying
goes. Helter-skelter shops inside
this shabby-chic collection of
houses are filled with affordable
treasures, especially for fans of
outrageous kitsch and funky
fashions.

🔲 HOUDINI'S MAGIC SHOP

☎ 798-4789; www.houdini.com; Forum Shops at Caesars Palace, 3500 Las Vegas Blvd S; 🕐 10am-11pm Sun-Thu, 10am-midnight Fri & Sat; Ⓜ Flamingo/Caesars Palace

The legendary escape artist's legacy lives on at this shop packed with gags, pranks and magic tricks. Tuxedoed magicians perform for free, and every purchase includes a free private lesson in the secretive back room. Look over the shop's mini museum of authentic Houdini memorabilia, including handcuffs.

🔲 LUSH

☎ 227-5874; www.lush.com; Mandalay Place, 3930 Las Vegas Blvd S; 🕐 10am-11pm Sun-Thu, 10am-midnight Fri & Sat; 🚌 Deuce

Be deliciously immersed back in your hotel room's bathtub with Lush's essential-oil-infused 'bath ballistics,' bubble bars and cocoa-butter bath melts, not to mention fresh, handmade pots of balms, cleansers and massage bars. Mostly natural and often organic, this is an eco-green beauty queen's dream.

🔲 RETRO VEGAS

☎ 384-2700; www.retro-vegas.com; 1211 S Main St; 🕐 11am-6pm Mon-Sat; 🚌 409

In the 18b Arts District (p14), this flamingo-pink antiques shop is a primo place for picking up mid-20th-century modern, art-deco and swingin' 1960s and '70s gems, from jewelry to home decor. Keep a sharp eye out for vintage Vegas souvenirs like casino-hotel ashtrays.

🔲 VIVA ELVIS OFFICIAL STORE

☎ 590-7111; www.arialasvegas.com; Aria, 3730 Las Vegas Blvd S; 🕐 10am-midnight Fri-Tue, 10am-8pm Wed & Thu; Ⓜ Flamingo/Caesars Palace

Near Cirque du Soleil's *Viva Elvis* theater (see p147), this fabulous shrine to the King of rock 'n' roll sells memorabilia you can't buy anywhere else, not even at Grace-land. Need a giant-sized Elvis pez dispenser or a diamond-encrusted TCB lightning-bolt replica ring? We thought so.

🔲 WEIRD & WONDERFUL

You can find quirky Atomic Age collectibles, books and movies at the Atomic Testing Museum (p74). Swoon over candelabras and life-sized photos of the legend himself at the Liberace Museum (p79).

🔲 BONANZA GIFTS

☎ 385-7359; www.worldslargest giftshop.com; 2440 Las Vegas Blvd S; 🕐 8am-midnight; Ⓜ Sahara

It's not the 'World's Largest Gift Shop' as it claims to be, but the truly terrible and guaranteed 100%

BEST ONLY-IN-VEGAS SHOPS
> Gamblers Book Shop (p90)
> Gamblers General Store (below)
> Gold & Silver Pawn (below)
> Rainbow Feather Dyeing Co (right)
> Viva Elvis Official Store (opposite)

tacky selection of only-in-Vegas souvenirs includes entire aisles of dice clocks, snow globes, slogan T-shirts, shot glasses and XXX gags. Beware that prices are higher here than downtown on Fremont St.

🏬 GAMBLERS GENERAL STORE
☎ 382-9903, 800-322-2447; www .gamblersgeneralstore.com; 800 S Main St; ⏰ 9am-6pm; 🚌 409
This authentic store has it all, from custom-made chips to roulette wheels and poker tables identical to those found in many casinos, plus Nevada's largest inventory of slot machines. It's perfect for cheapo gifts like decks of cards once used in real-life Vegas casinos.

🏬 GOLD & SILVER PAWN
☎ 385-7912; http://gspawn.com; 713 Las Vegas Blvd S; ⏰ 24hr; 🚌 Deuce
As seen on the reality-TV hit series *Pawn Stars* (see p75), this humble-looking storefront has untold treasures inside, from Wild West shotguns and restored 1950s classic cars to vintage Vegas

casino and autographed star memorabilia. Line up outside by the red-velvet rope.

🏬 GUN STORE
☎ 454-1110; www.thegunstorelas vegas.com; 2900 E Tropicana Ave; ⏰ 9am-6:30pm; 🚌 201
Attention wannabe action heroes. If you're dying to fire off a sub-machine gun or feel the heft of a Beretta, Colt or Glock in your hot little hands, visit this high-powered shop with an indoor video training range. Tuesday is ladies' day.

🏬 RAINBOW FEATHER DYEING CO
☎ 598-0988; www.rainbowfeatherco .com; 1036 S Main St; ⏰ 9am-4pm Mon-Fri, 9am-1pm Sat; 🚌 409
Where to satisfy that boa fetish? Need turkey, chicken, duck, goose, pheasant, ostrich or peacock quills? Rainbow stocks a positively fabulous selection of fine feathers and showgirl fans in every possible hue.

🏬 SERGE'S SHOWGIRL WIGS
☎ 732-1015, 800-947-9447; www.show girlwigs.com; Commercial Center, 953 E Sahara Ave; ⏰ 10am-5:30pm Mon-Sat; 🚌 204
In a trashy strip mall east of the Sahara casino hotel, Serge's friendly staff of stylists help Vegas showgirls and drag queens (and even little ol' you) find their inner glamour girl.

⊞ EAT

Sin City is studded with star chefs, and today's foodie scene is on fire. The recent invasion of the Strip by French chefs, most notably Guy Savoy, Joël Robuchon and Pierre Gagnaire, is just the latest notch in the city's climb toward ever more sophisticated epicurean experiences.

After Wolfgang Puck brought Spago to Caesars Palace in 1992, celebrity American chefs opened branches at every megaresort. Geniuses of the kitchen who have leapt onto the Strip include Emeril Legasse, Mario Batali, Michael Mina, Bobby Flay, Rick Moonen and Susan Feniger. However, cheap buffets and meal deals still exist, mostly downtown and at less glitzy Strip addresses.

Every major casino hotel has a 24-hour cafe, typically offering graveyard specials after midnight. Weekend champagne brunch buffets (10:30am to 3:30pm) are a hot ticket. Lunch is between 11:30am and 2:30pm. Dinner is from 5pm to 10pm Sunday through Thursday, and to 11pm on Friday and Saturday nights.

Almost every restaurant menu on the Strip offers a few creative vegetarian appetizers and side dishes, which you can easily combine into a full meal. Restaurants with a particularly good vegetarian selection have been identified in the individual reviews with the symbol Ⓥ .

Book tables as far in advance as you can for pricier restaurants. Reservations at the biggest names are crucial, especially on weekends. At the most famous places, jackets may be required for men. **OpenTable** (www .opentable.com) is a free online booking service. Immediate bar seating is often available.

The standard gratuity is 15% to 20% before tax. A service charge of 15% to 18% is often added for groups of six or more; don't double-tip.

Top Left Get your burgers fresh at Stripburger (p106) **Bottom Left** Don't mess around with the hefty sandwiches at Canter's Deli (p115)

THE STRIP

For tips on Vegas' belly-busting buffets, turn to p171.

BELLAGIO

The Bellagio's stable of culinary heavyweights has started showing its age. For reservations, visit www.bellagio.com or call ☎ 866-259-7111. Young children are not permitted at some top-end restaurants.

THE BUFFET

Buffet $$

☎ 693-7111; Bellagio, 3600 Las Vegas Blvd S; ⏲ 7am-10pm, champagne brunch 7am-4pm Sat & Sun; Ⓜ Bally's/Paris; Ⓥ ♿

The Bellagio competes for top honors for Vegas' best live-action buffet. The sumptuous all-you-can-eat spread includes seafood and uncountable creative dishes from all around the globe. Go for lunch, which is the best value.

FIX

Modern American $$

☎ 693-8300; www.lightgroup.com; Bellagio, 3600 Las Vegas Blvd S; ⏲ 5pm-midnight Sun-Thu, 5pm-2am Fri & Sat; Ⓜ Bally's/Paris

It's a perfect preclubbing launch pad, or just the venue for eyeing celebs and the casino floor. This trendy, high-flying kitchen makes gourmet comfort-food good-

MEAL COSTS

The pricing symbols used in this book indicate the cost of a main dinner course, excluding tax, tips or drinks.

$	under $15
$$	$15-50
$$$	over $50

ies such as lobster tacos, Kobe beef sliders with spiced fries and choco-java 'shake & cake.' Reservations recommended at Fix and its sister Japanese restaurant and sushi bar Yellowtail.

JEAN-PHILIPPE PATISSERIE

French $

☎ 693-7111; Spa Tower, Bellagio, 3600 Las Vegas Blvd S; items $5-10; ⏲ 7am-11pm Mon-Thu, 7am-midnight Fri-Sun; Ⓜ Bally's/Paris

The world's largest chocolate fountain cascades inside this champion pastrymaker's shop, known for its fantastic sorbets, gelatos and chocolate confections. Sugar-free sweets don't disappoint either.

OLIVES

Mediterranean $$

☎ 693-8181; www.toddenglish.com; Via Bellagio, Bellagio, 3600 Las Vegas Blvd S; ⏲ 11am-2:45pm & 5-10:30pm; Ⓜ Bally's/Paris; Ⓥ

East Coast chef Todd English pays homage to the ancient life-giving fruit. Flatbread pizzas, house-made pastas and flame-licked meats get top billing. The chef's table faces a bustling open kitchen, while the patio tables overlook Lake Como. There's a good wine list, and flamboyant desserts. Reservations here are necessary.

🍴 CAESARS PALACE & FORUM SHOPS
Make reservations for dining with the gods at www.caesarspalace .com, or call ☎ 731-7731 or ☎ 877-346-4642. Wolfgang Puck's Spago ($$) is inside the Forum Shops (p92).

🍴 BRADLEY OGDEN
Modern American $$$
☎ 731-7413; www.larkcreek.com; opposite Colosseum, Caesars Palace, 3570 Las Vegas Blvd S; ⏰ 5-11pm Wed-Sun; Ⓜ Flamingo/Caesars Palace
With farm-fresh fare, this restaurant delivers nouveau takes on American classics, such as blue-cheese soufflés, bison tenderloin and New England crab with dollops of coconut foam. Reservations advised.

🍴 CYPRESS STREET MARKETPLACE
Fast Food $
☎ 731-7110; opposite Colosseum, Caesars Palace, 3570 Las Vegas Blvd S; ⏰ 11am-11pm; Ⓜ Flamingo/Caesars Palace; Ⓥ ♿

Conveniently charge those fresh, made-to-order pizzas and salads, global wraps, Asian stir-fries and southern barbecue, along with beer, wine and health drinks, to a 'smart' card, then pay upon exiting. Courtyard tables perch happily over the casino floor.

🍴 MESA GRILL
Southwestern $$
☎ 731-7731; www.mesagrill.com/las vegas; opposite Colosseum, Caesars Palace, 3570 Las Vegas Blvd S; ⏰ 11am-2:30pm Mon-Fri, 10:30am-3pm Sat & Sun, 5-11pm daily; Ⓜ Flamingo/Caesars Palace; Ⓥ
While the star New York chef doesn't cook on the premises, his bold signature menu of Southwestern fusion fare lives up to the hype, whether it's a sweet potato tamale with crushed pecan butter, blue-corn pancakes or spice-rubbed pork tenderloin.

🍴 PAYARD BISTRO
French $$
☎ 731-7292; www.payard.com; Caesars Palace, 3570 Las Vegas Blvd S; ⏰ 6:30am-3pm; Ⓜ Flamingo/Caesars Palace
Third-generation chef and chocolatier Françoise Payard re-creates classic French bistro tastes as rich as the handcrafted woodwork, leather banquettes and crystal chandelier in the bright dining room. Out front is a divine

pâtisserie (🕑 6:30am-11pm) and espresso bar for quick pick-me-ups.

🍴 RESTAURANT GUY SAVOY
French $$$
☎ 731-7731; www.guysavoy.com; 2nd
fl, Augustus Tower, Caesars Palace, 3570
Las Vegas Blvd S; 🕑 5:30-9:30pm Wed-
Sun; Ⓜ Flamingo/Caesars Palace
With Strip-view windows over-
looking Caesars' Roman Plaza,
this intimate dining room is the
only US endeavor of three-star
Michelin chef Guy Savoy. Both
the culinary concepts and the
prices reach heavenly heights.
Pop by the Bubble Bar for
champagne flights and delicate
small plates such as artichoke and
black-truffle soup. Jacket and tie
required. Reservations essential
but difficult to get.

🍴 SERENDIPITY 3
American $$
☎ 731-7110; www.serendipity3.com;
outside Caesars Palace, 3570 Las Vegas
Blvd S; 🕑 11am-11pm Mon-Thu, 11am-
midnight Fri, 9am-midnight Sat, 9am-
11pm Sun; Ⓜ Flamingo/Caesars Palace
At this pink candy-striped soda
fountain, sink your sweet tooth
into frozen hot chocolate and
opulent ice-cream sundaes. Skip
the so-so grill menu.

🍴 CITYCENTER
CityCenter's Aria casino resort,
the Mandarin Oriental hotel and
Crystals shopping mall all draw
epicureans.

🍴 AMERICAN FISH
Seafood $$
☎ 590-8610; www.michaelmina.net;
Aria, 3730 Las Vegas Blvd S; 🕑 5-
10:30pm Wed-Mon; 🚌 Deuce
From the fertile mind of chef
Michael Mina, Aria's upstairs sea-
food house keeps things simple.
Choose your fish cooked one of
four elemental ways: poached,
baked in sea salt, grilled or wood-
smoked. Delicate shellfish appetiz-
ers such as abalone stew, seasonal
garden vegetable sides and ex-
quisite cocktails are all stand-outs.
Reservations recommended.

🍴 JEAN-GEORGES STEAKHOUSE
Steakhouse $$$
☎ 590-7111; Aria, 3730 Las Vegas Blvd S;
🕑 5-11:30pm; 🚌 Deuce

HIGH-ROLLER TABLES ON THE STRIP
> Alex (p117)
> Joël Robuchon (p108)
> Restaurant Guy Savoy (left)
> Tao (p116)
> Twist by Pierre Gagnaire (opposite)

Fusing the most eclectic tastes from East and West, this Michelin-starred chef's serious steakhouse is extraordinary. Just upstairs from Aria's casino, soothingly low lighting and squeezed-together tables don't distract too much from inventive tastes like black-truffle fritters, rice-cracker-crusted tuna or soy-glazed short ribs, along with bone-in filet mignon. Reservations essential.

🍽 JULIAN SERRANO
Mediterranean $$
☎ 590-8520; Aria, 3730 Las Vegas Blvd S; ⏲ 11am-11pm; 🚌 Deuce
A splash of sunset colors stolen straight from Ibiza enlivens this sociable tapas bar and restaurant, just off Aria's hotel lobby. Start off with sangria, then dance through the French and Spanish tapas menu, from imported cured hams and goat-cheese-stuffed peppers to hot skillets of mixed seafood paella. Reservations recommended.

🍽 SAGE
Modern American $$
☎ 877-230-2742; www.arialasvegas.com; Aria, 3730 Las Vegas Blvd S; ⏲ 5-11pm Mon-Sat; 🚌 Deuce; Ⓥ
Chef Shawn McClain brings his Midwestern farm-to-table cuisine to the Strip. The gorgeous backlit bar mural almost steals

the scene, but creative twists on meat-and-potatoes classics and outside-the-box vegetarian offerings shine. After dinner, sip an absinthe. Reservations recommended.

🍽 SOCIAL HOUSE
Pan-Asian $$
☎ 736-1122; www.socialhouselv.com; Crystals, 3720 Las Vegas Blvd S; ⏲ 5-10pm Sun-Thu, 1-4:30pm & 5-11pm Fri & Sat; 🚌 Deuce
You won't find a sexier sushi bar and pan-Asian grill anywhere on the Strip. Low-slung tatami cushions, faded Japanese woodblock prints and a sky terrace inside Crystals mall all add up to a seductively date-worthy atmosphere. Don't be surprised to spot a Hollywood celeb here.

🍽 TWIST BY PIERRE GAGNAIRE
French $$$
☎ 888-881-9367; Mandarin Oriental, 3752 Las Vegas Blvd S; ⏲ 6-10pm Tue-Sat; 🚌 Deuce
If Twist's sparkling nighttime Strip views don't make you gasp, the high-modern French cuisine by this three-star Michelin chef just might. Seasonal tasting menus ($185) range from squid-ink gnocchetti topped by carrot gelée or langoustine with seaweed ice cubes to asparagus ice cream with

tart green apples. Reservations essential.

🍴 WOLFGANG PUCK PIZZERIA & CUCINA
Italian $$

☎ 238-1000; www.wolfgangpuck.com; Crystals, 3720 Las Vegas Blvd S; ☽ 5-10pm Sun-Thu, 5-11pm Fri & Sat; 🚌 Deuce; Ⓥ

Pulling another rabbit out of his chef's hat, Wolfgang Puck has landed this primo terrace upstairs at Crystals mall. Crispy, creative pizzas are the stars of the menu, or stick your knife into modern Cal-Italian classics like ricotta gnocchi, wild mushroom ravioli or eggplant parmesan. A hand-picked wine list includes both European and American varietals.

🍴 FASHION SHOW

For authentic Italian-style scoops, rainbow-colored Gelato Cafe ($) is a sweet spot.

🍴 STRIPBURGER
American $

☎ 737-8747; http://lasvegasstripburger.com; street level, Fashion Show, 3200 Las Vegas Blvd S; ☽ 11:30am-midnight; 🚌 Ace Gold; 🚼

A shiny, silver-roofed open-air diner in the round serves up all-natural beef, chicken, turkey and veggie burgers, with chili-spiked 'atomic' cheese fries on the side. Draft microbrews, thick milk-shakes and chocolate cake are served, too.

Make a reservation for upscale wining and dining at Aureole

LUXOR

For a zingy, fusion-flavored meal in sexy surrounds, queue for celeb chef Kerry Simon's CatHouse ($$).

TACOS & TEQUILA
Mexican $

☎ 262-5225; www.tacosandtequilalv.com; Luxor, 3900 Las Vegas Blvd S; ⏱ 11am-11pm; 🚌 Deuce
Edgy industrial design and a mischievously black-curtained photo booth pull rock 'n' roll crowds upstairs to this insanely popular taquería. Hot-tamale bartenders and tequila temptresses pour shots and pitchers of sangria, while Sunday brunch brings live mariachi bands.

MANDALAY BAY & MANDALAY PLACE
For table reservations, click to www.mandalaybay.com or call ☎ 632-7200.

AUREOLE
Modern American $$$

☎ 632-7401; www.aureolelv.com; Mandalay Bay, 3950 Las Vegas Blvd S; ⏱ 5:30-10:30pm, wine-tower lounge 5:30pm-midnight; 🚌 Deuce
Chef Charlie Palmer's seasonally inspired tasting menus (from $95), which show off dishes like saffron seafood chowder and maple-nut baklava, are not always artfully executed. But it's worth ordering wine just to watch catsuit-clad 'wine angels' ascend the four-story tower. Extensive wine list, upscale dress. Reservations essential.

HUSSONG'S CANTINA
Mexican $

☎ 553-0123; www.hussongslasvegas.com; Mandalay Place, 3930 Las Vegas Blvd S; ⏱ 11am-11pm Sun-Thu, 11am-midnight Fri & Sat, bar 11am-2am daily; 🚌 Deuce
This Baja-style cantina brings rowdy, south-of-the-border attitude to Mandalay Bay's mall. The original Hussong's down in Ensenada claims to have invented the margarita, so trust the drinks here will be knock-outs, especially when served in skull-shaped glasses. Tacos, nachos, burritos and other Mexican-American standards make up the wooden signboard's menu.

RM SEAFOOD
Seafood $$$

☎ 632-9300; www.rmseafood.com; Mandalay Place, 3930 Las Vegas Blvd S; ⏱ restaurant 5:30-10pm Tue-Sat, cafe 11:30am-11pm daily; 🚌 Deuce
New York chef Rick Moonen takes a dual approach to the sustainable catch of the day. Upstairs in the restaurant, relish haute American seafood dinners. The

BEST STEAKHOUSES

Vegas has hundreds of places to get a hunk of burnin' red meat. Extra props go to the following steakhouses:
> Cut (Palazzo; p111)
> Craftsteak (MGM Grand; right)
> Jean-Georges Steakhouse (p104)
> N9NE (Palms; p127)
> Vic & Anthony's (Golden Nugget; p121)

downstairs cafe, furnished with rich mahogany booths, offers a more expansive menu, a raw shell-fish and sushi bar, and a unique 'biscuit bar' serving warm seafood salads.

STRIPSTEAK
Steakhouse/Seafood $$$

☎ 632-7414; www.michaelmina.net; Mandalay Bay, 3950 Las Vegas Blvd S; ⏰ 5:30-11pm; 🚌 Deuce

Famed for his seafood restaurants, chef Michael Mina has made a graceful debut into the cut-throat world of Vegas steakhouses. Here minimalist modern design is warmed by earth tones, and an exceptional menu of Angus and Kobe beef delightfully detours from tradition, with the likes of duck-fat fries, spicy green-papaya salad and tomato-dusted red-onion rings on the side. Reservations recommended.

 ### MGM GRAND

For reservations, click to www.mgmgrand.com or call ☎ 877-793-7111. Palatable options include Fiamma Trattoria & Bar ($$) for modish Italian, and 'wichcraft ($) for grab-and-go sandwiches.

CRAFTSTEAK
Steakhouse/Seafood $$$

☎ 891-7318; www.craftrestaurant.com; Studio Walk, MGM Grand, 3799 Las Vegas Blvd S; ⏰ 5:30-10pm Sun-Thu, 5:30-10:30pm Fri & Sat; Ⓜ MGM Grand

What this contemporary, richly wood-laden space may lack in exclusivity it makes up for with an intriguing menu of grass-fed vs grain-fed strip steaks, grilled bison, braised duck confit and a bounty from the sea: regional American oysters, Russian caviar and Australian lobster tail. There's a three-course tasting menu (from $110).

JOËL ROBUCHON
French $$$

☎ 891-7925; www.joel-robuchon.com; MGM Grand, 3799 Las Vegas Blvd S; ⏰ 5:30-10pm Sun-Thu, 5:30-10:30pm Fri & Sat; Ⓜ MGM Grand

The acclaimed 'Chef of the Cen-tury' leads the pack in the French invasion of Las Vegas. Adjacent to the Mansion, a high-rollers' gaming area, plush dining rooms done up in leather and velvet imitate 1930s Paris. There are complex seasonal tasting menus ($85 to $385). Reservations essential but difficult to get. At less-expensive L'Atelier de Joël Robuchon ($$$) next door, bar seats front an exhibition kitchen.

🍽 SEABLUE
Seafood $$$
☎ 891-3486; www.michaelmina.net; MGM Grand, 3799 Las Vegas Blvd S; 🕑 5:30-10pm Sun-Thu, 5:30-10:30pm Fri & Sat; Ⓜ MGM Grand
Anything from Nantucket Bay scallops to Gulf shrimp to Manila clams comes raw, fried, steamed and roasted out of two exhibition kitchens. Create your own mix-and-match salads from a long list of farm-fresh ingredients, and then swallow a fanciful lobster corn dog.

🍽 SHIBUYA
Japanese $$$
☎ 891-3001; Studio Walk, MGM Grand, 3799 Las Vegas Blvd S; 🕑 5-10pm Sun-Thu, 5-10:30pm Fri & Sat; Ⓜ MGM Grand
A stellar sake cellar, art spreading behind the sushi bar and tastebud-awakening appetizers, such as garlic-rubbed yellowtail with citrus juice and black-truffle oil, and oysters spiked with *ponzu* sauce.

Teppanyaki set menus come with lobster-miso or mushroom soup.

🍽 WOLFGANG PUCK BAR & GRILL
Italian $$
☎ 891-3000; www.wolfgangpuck .com; MGM Grand, 3799 Las Vegas Blvd S; 🕑 11:30am-10:30pm Sun-Thu, 11:30am-11:30pm Fri & Sat; Ⓜ MGM Grand; Ⓥ
California flair pervades this ultra-contemporary bistro just off the casino floor. The truffled potato chips with blue cheese, skirt steak skewers with celery salad, wood-fired pizzas and ricotta gnocchi with sweet fennel sausage thrill, just like the New World wine list.

🍴 MIRAGE

For reservations, go to www. mirage.com or call ☎ 866-339-4566. Some savory options include Stack ($$), the look-alike of Fix (p102), and Carnegie Deli ($$), where everything comes hugely oversized.

🍽 BLT BURGER
American $
☎ 792-7888; www.bltburger.com; Mirage, 3400 Las Vegas Blvd S; 🕑 11am-2am Sun-Thu, 10am-4am Fri & Sat; Ⓜ Harrah's/Imperial Palace
Here, French-trained NYC chef Laurent Tourondel grills up haute

Black Angus beef, lamb and veggie burgers with all the trimmings, plus there are almost three dozen microbrews, liqueur-spiked 'adult' milkshakes, crisp sweet-potato fries and peanut-buttery s'mores for dessert. Beautiful mod diner-style furnishings have a background of enormous black-and-white photo murals that show off Nevada's desert and snowy mountains.

🍴 JAPONAIS
Pan-Asian $$
☎ 792-7979; www.japonaislasvegas.com; Mirage, 3400 Las Vegas Blvd S; ⏰ 5-10pm Sun-Thu, 5-11pm Fri & Sat, lounge noon-1am Mon-Wed, noon-2am Thu & Fri; Ⓜ Harrah's/Imperial Palace

This sushi and sake bar is designed for socializing. While panko-crusted crab cakes and grilled Kobe beef may not always hit the right notes, a theatrical lipstick-red dining room with a sculpted wood ceiling and a casino-view lounge with gossamer drapes do.

🍴 NEW YORK–NEW YORK
Dig into upscale country Irish cooking at Nine Fine Irishmen ($$). Upstairs on the mezzanine level is a cluster of fast-food stands: Nathan's famous hot dogs, Schrafft's ice cream, Tropicana juice smoothies and 99¢ cups of coffee.

🍴 IL FORNAIO
Italian $$
☎ 650-6500; www.ilfornaio.com; New York–New York, 3790 Las Vegas Blvd S; ⏰ 7:30-10:30am & 11:30am-midnight; Ⓜ MGM Grand; Ⓥ

Feast on wood-fired pizzas, salads and pastas, or make a meal of the antipasti platter with scallops wrapped in pancetta, baked eggplant, truffled cheeses and more. Delectable, fresh-baked breakfast goodies such as lemon-pecan scones are also available at **Il Fornaio Paneterria** (⏰ 6am-7:30pm), near the hotel lobby.

🍴 VILLAGE EATERIES
Fast Food $
☎ 740-6969; www.nynyhotelcasino.com; New York–New York, 3790 Las Vegas Blvd S; ⏰ daily, hours vary; Ⓜ MGM Grand; Ⓥ ♿

The cobblestone streets of NY–NY's imitation Greenwich Village are bursting with tasty, wallet-saving options: Greenberg's Deli, authentic down to the egg-cream sodas; Fulton's Original Fish Frye for hot fish and chips; Gonzalez Y Gonzalez, a tequila-soaked Tex-Mex cantina; Jody Maroni's Sausage Kingdom grilling haute dogs; and Chin Chin Café, serving dim sum appetizers and other quick-fix Chinese-American dishes.

Savor the spiciness of Dos Caminos

 PALAZZO

For reservations, click to www
.palazzolasvegas.com or call
☎ 607-7777.

CUT
Steakhouse $$$
☎ 607-6300; www.wolfgangpuck.com;
**Shoppes at the Palazzo, 3327 Las Vegas
Blvd S;** ⏰ 5:30-10pm Sun-Thu, 5:30-
11pm Fri & Sat, lounge 5pm-1am daily;
Ⓜ **Harrah's/Imperial Palace**
Peripatetic Wolfgang Puck strikes
again, and this time he's on fire –
it's 1200°F in the broiler, to be
exact. Modern earth-toned
furnishings with stainless-steel
accents and dried-flower arrange-
ments complement a surprisingly
smart menu, which dares to infuse
Indian spices into Kobe beef, and
accompanies Nebraska corn-fed
steaks with Argentinean chimi-
churri sauce or Point Reyes blue
cheese. Reservations essential.

DOS CAMINOS
Mexican $$
☎ 577-9600; www.brguestrestaurants
.com; **Palazzo, 3325 Las Vegas Blvd S;**
⏰ 11am-11pm Sun-Thu, 11am-midnight
Fri & Sat; Ⓜ **Harrah's/Imperial Palace**
Whether you've got a boisterous
party or an intimate date, this sex-
ily reinvented Mexican restaurant
is the ideal place for lounging,
with its low-slung tables and

sofas and a long list of specialty cocktails and tequila flights. Linger over *queso* fondues, spicy seafood seviche and chili-rubbed meats *a la parilla* (from the grill). Weekend brunch brings tacos, *huevos* (eggs) and blueberry-corn pancakes.

🍴 ESPRESSAMENTE ILLY
Fast Food $

☎ 869-2233; www.palazzolasvegas .com; Shoppes at the Palazzo, 3327 Las Vegas Blvd S; 🕑 6am-midnight Sun-Thu, 6am-1am Fri & Sat; Ⓜ Harrah's/Imperial Palace

A whiff of real Italian espresso leads you inside this brightly lit cafe. House-made panini, dessert crepes and over four dozen flavors of artisan gelato provide the sugar rush you'll need to attack the racks nearby at Barneys New York (p94). Beware of the annoying, hidden 'dine-in' surcharge.

🍴 FIRST FOOD & BAR
American $$

☎ 607-3478; www.firstfoodandbar. com; Shoppes at the Palazzo, 3327 Las Vegas Blvd S; 🕑 11am-1am Sun-Thu, 11am-4am Fri & Sat; Ⓜ Harrah's/Imperial Palace

Foodies will salivate over this haute bar and grill with a seriously creative edge. Order up Philly cheesesteak dumplings, Dr Pepper ribs with cheesy grits or a cotton-candy-flavored cocktail. Metallic

industrial design, vintage-goth furnishings and carpeting with tattoo patterns all look especially sexy after midnight, when the clubbing crowd takes over.

🍴 MORELS
Steakhouse/Seafood $$$

☎ 607-6333; www.palazzolasvegas .com; Palazzo, 3325 Las Vegas Blvd S; 🕑 11:30am-11pm Mon-Thu, 11:30am-midnight Fri & Sat, 11:30am-10pm Sun; Ⓜ Harrah's/Imperial Palace

Another LA imported steakhouse, bejeweled Morels has a few secret weapons: gorgeous alfresco patio seating elevated above the Strip, an ice seafood bar, an artisanal cheese and charcuterie meat bar, and a wine-dispensing system that lets you sip just a glass of thousand-dollar French and Californian vintages. Impeccable service. Reservations recommended.

🍴 SUSHISAMBA
Japanese/South American $$

☎ 607-0700; www.sushisamba.com; Shoppes at the Palazzo, 3327 Las Vegas Blvd S; 🕑 11:30am-4pm daily, 5pm-1am Sun-Wed, 5pm-2am Thu-Sat; Ⓜ Harrah's/Imperial Palace

With the flouncy colors of Rio and martial-arts flicks digitally projected onto the walls, SushiSamba presents a chic, sleek integration of Peruvian, Brazilian and Japanese cuisine, such as flawlessly grilled *robata* and churrasco meats, marinated sashimi seviche spiked with citrus and chilies, or delicately done tempura boxes with dipping sauces. And whoa, the sake list is encyclopedic. Reservations strongly recommended.

🍴 TABLE 10
Steakhouse/Seafood $$
☎ 607-6363; www.emerils.com; Shoppes at the Palazzo, 3327 Las Vegas Blvd S; ⏰ 11am-11pm Sun-Thu, 11am-midnight Fri & Sat; Ⓜ Harrah's/Imperial Palace

Named after a prime spot at Emeril Legasse's flagship restaurant in N'awlins, Table 10 offers a New American take on classics such as lobster pot pie, spinach salad and dry-aged Angus ribeye steaks. Over-the-top desserts include white-chocolate malasadas rolled in cinnamon-sugar with vanilla-

---

BEST TABLES WITH A VIEW
When the panorama is important and price is not, ascend to the the Mandarin Oriental's **Twist by Pierre Gagnaire** (p105), the Palms' **Alizé** (p125) or the Stratosphere Tower's **Top of the World** (p115). For patios with Strip views, nab a table at Paris' **Mon Ami Gabi** (right) or the Palazzo's **Morels** (opposite).

---

bean crème anglaise. Reservations recommended.

🍴 PARIS LAS VEGAS
Other options include the Rue de la Paix's La Creperie ($).

🍴 LE VILLAGE BUFFET
Buffet $$
☎ 946-7000; www.parislasvegas.com; Rue de la Paix, Paris Las Vegas, 3655 Las Vegas Blvd S; ⏰ 7am-10pm; Ⓜ Bally's/Paris; Ⓥ ♿

Fruit and cheeses, cracked crab legs and a toasty range of breads and pastries make this arguably the best-value buffet on the Strip. Distinct cooking stations are themed by France's various regions. Breakfasts are *magnifique*, especially the Sunday champagne brunch.

🍴 MON AMI GABI
French $$
☎ 944-4224; www.monamigabi.com; Paris Las Vegas, 3655 Las Vegas Blvd S; ⏰ 7am-11pm Sun-Fri, 7am-midnight Sat; Ⓜ Bally's/Paris

Think *très* charming Champs Élysées bistro. Breezy patio tables in the shadow of the Eiffel Tower are *parfait* for alfresco dining and people-watching. Though the French fare is far from *magnifique*, they've got classic steak frites; vegetarian crepes, quiches and salads;

special gluten-free selections; and a respectable wine list. Reservations recommended.

 PLANET HOLLYWOOD

The Earl of Sandwich ($) and next-door Miracle Mile Shops (p94) offer cheaper eats.

 KOI
Sushi $$

☎ 454-4555; www.planethollywood resort.com; upstairs, Planet Hollywood, 3667 Las Vegas Blvd S; ⏱ 5:30-10:30pm Sun-Thu, 5:30-11:30pm Fri & Sat; Ⓜ Bally's/Paris

Although the paparazzi won't lunge at you outside the front door like at the ubercool LA hot spot of the same name, this sushi bar is making waves in the desert (move over, Nobu). Bite into yellowtail carpaccio and down a blood-orange sunset cosmo cocktail.

PINK'S
Fast Food $

☎ 785-5555; www.pinkshollywood. com; Planet Hollywood, 3667 Las Vegas Blvd S; ⏱ 10:30am-midnight Sun-Thu, 10:30am-3am Fri & Sat; Ⓜ Bally's/Paris

From Los Angeles, this celebrity-endorsed 'haute dog' stand serves up sloppy, chili-cheese, jalapeño and guacamole-topped dogs for late-night noshing. It's far from

gourmet, but it helps soak up all that booze. Sunny sidewalk patio tables overlooking the Strip are often packed.

SPICE MARKET BUFFET
Buffet $$

☎ 785-5555; www.planethollywood resort.com; downstairs, Planet Hollywood, 3667 Las Vegas Blvd S; ⏱ 7am-10pm; Ⓜ Bally's/Paris

Middle Eastern specialties are thrown into the global mix at this jewel of a five-star buffet, with delectable desserts. Attentive service and live-action cooking stations justify the often very long waits to be seated.

STRIP HOUSE
Steakhouse $$$

☎ 737-5200; www.planethollywood resort.com; upstairs, Planet Hollywood, 3667 Las Vegas Blvd S; ⏱ 5-11pm Sun-Thu, 5pm-midnight Fri & Sat; Ⓜ Bally's/Paris

Boudoir lamps, leather banquettes and vintage erotic art prints set the mood at this sultry steakhouse, an aspiring celeb hangout. Start off with the garlic bread and Gorgonzola fondue, then fork into the broiler steaks and attack the 24-layer chocolate cake. Eclectic, sommelier-inspired wine list. Reservations here are recommended.

STRATOSPHERE

TOP OF THE WORLD

American $$$

☎ 380-7711; www.topoftheworldlv
.com; Stratosphere, 2000 Las Vegas Blvd
S; ⏱ 11am-10:30pm Sun-Thu, 11am-
11pm Fri & Sat; Ⓜ Sahara

While taking in the cloud-level
views at this dressy, revolving,
romantic roost perched atop the
Stratosphere Tower (p84), relish
impeccable service and satisfying
if overpriced mains such as wild
king salmon or chateaubriand for
two. Reservations recommended
for lunch, required for dinner.
Excellent wine list.

TI (TREASURE ISLAND)

For reservations, visit www
.treasureisland.com or call ☎ 866-
286-3809. Phở at the Coffee Shop
($) preps Vietnamese noodle soup
that won't leave you hungry.

CANTER'S DELI

Jewish Deli $

☎ 894-7111; www.cantersdeli.com; TI
(Treasure Island), 3300 Las Vegas Blvd S;
⏱ 11am-midnight; 🚌 Deuce

What did Canter's bring over the
state line from its landmark LA
delicatessen? You guessed it: the
infamously gruff service. Steal a
seat at the stainless-steel counter
or slide into a super-mod booth,

then settle back for authentic deli
fare that's almost as good as it gets.

ISLA MEXICAN KITCHEN

Mexican $$

☎ 894-7223; www.treasureisland.com;
TI (Treasure Island), 3300 Las Vegas Blvd
S; ⏱ 4-10pm Sun-Thu, 4-11pm Fri & Sat;
🚌 Deuce

Bold art enlivens the walls of this
invention by Mexican-born chef
Richard Sandoval, who creates
a fusion of south-of-the-border
tastes, such as guacamole with a
twist of mint, and lobster spiked
with serrano chilies. Call on Isla's
tequila goddess to help decipher
the bounteous menu of agave
elixirs.

Sample deli favorites at Canter's

LAS VEGAS

EAT

🍴 VENETIAN & GRAND CANAL SHOPPES

This bite of Italy offers a dizzying lineup of dining destinations, but not all excel. Reservations (☎ 877-883-6423; www.venetian.com) are a must for top-end dining rooms. Canyon Ranch Café & Grill ($$) serves healthy cuisine inside the spa (p148), while French-flavored Bouchon Bakery ($) is popular for patisserie bites.

🍴 B&B RISTORANTE
Italian $$
☎ 266-9977; www.mariobatali.com; Venetian, 3355 Las Vegas Blvd S; 🕒 5-11pm; M Harrah's/Imperial Palace
From thriving Italian restaurateur and TV chef Mario Batali and his winemaking partner (the other 'B'), this risk-taking restaurant delivers eccentric yet tantalizing dishes, such as beef-cheek ravioli, baby red-oak leaf salad with blood-orange dressing and lamb's brains with lemon and sage. Extravagant Eurocentric wine list. Reservations strongly recommended.

🍴 BOUCHON
French $$
☎ 414-6200; www.bouchonbistro.com; Venetian, 3355 Las Vegas Blvd S; 🕒 7-10:30am Mon-Fri, 8am-2pm Sat & Sun, 5-10pm daily; M Harrah's/Imperial Palace

Napa Valley wunderkind Thomas Keller's rendition of a Lyonnaise bistro features a seasonal menu of French classics. The poolside setting complements the oyster bar and an extensive raw seafood selection. Decadent breakfasts and brunches, imported cheeses and a superb French and Californian wine list all make an appearance. Service has its ups and downs.

🍴 POSTRIO
Italian $$
☎ 796-1110; www.wolfgangpuck.com; Grand Canal Shoppes, Venetian, 3377 Las Vegas Blvd S; 🕒 11am-10pm Sun-Thu, 11am-10:30pm Fri & Sat; M Harrah's/Imperial Palace; 🔊
This offshoot of Wolfgang Puck's San Francisco original features playful signature dishes; devotees can't get enough of the wood-oven-baked pizzas, pastas and rich desserts. Designed for people-watching, the patio always beats the stuffy restaurant. Interesting wine list.

🍴 TAO
Pan-Asian $$$
☎ 388-8338; www.taolasvegas.com; Grand Canal Shoppes, Venetian, 3377 Las Vegas Blvd S; 🕒 5pm-midnight Sun-Thu, 5pm-1am Fri & Sat; M Harrah's/Imperial Palace
Feng-shui design pervades this over-the-top bistro, where a

ginormous Buddha floats above an infinity pool. Tableside dim sum service uses traditional carts, or feast on filet mignon with udon noodles or Peking duck. A full bar stocks premium sake labels. Reservations essential, but difficult to score. Dress to impress, as it's a launching pad for Tao nightclub (p144).

WYNN & ENCORE

Reservations (call ☎ 248-3463 or 888-352-3463) and upscale dress are highly recommended.

🍴 ALEX

French/Mediterranean $$$
☎ 770-3463; Wynn, 3131 Las Vegas Blvd S; 🕑 6-10pm Wed-Sun; 🚌 Ace Gold
Award-winning chef Alessandro Stratta stretches his wings at this haute French Riviera restaurant, with wildly successful high-concept dishes such as frog legs with garlic confit and shellfish with pink grapefruit and sea urchin. The pastry chef also triumphs. Reservations are essential, and jackets are suggested for men.

🍴 THE BUFFET

Buffet $$
☎ 770-3463; www.wynnlasvegas.com; Wynn, 3131 Las Vegas Blvd S; 🕑 8am-10pm Sun-Thu, 8am-10:30pm Fri & Sat; 🚌 Ace Gold

Wynn's buffet is an uplifting experience, with live-action stations; hot dishes such as tangy barbecue, prime rib and wood-fired pizzas; and some of the freshest fruit, salads and seafood seviche in town. Delicate desserts and pastries tempt.

🍴 SINATRA

Italian $$
☎ 248-3463; Encore, 3131 Las Vegas Blvd S; 🕑 5:30-10pm; 🚌 Deuce
Ol' Blue Eyes would've felt right at home in these posh casino surrounds, with gorgeous chandeliers, banquettes, classical statuary and garden views. The kitchen delivers a mix of heart-warming and sophisticated Italian-American classics, from lasagne bolognese and octopus affogato to osso bucco 'My Way' and good ol' spaghetti and clams with red sauce. Reservations recommended.

🍴 STRATTA

Italian $$
☎ 770-3463; www.wynnlasvegas.com; Wynn, 3131 Las Vegas Blvd S; 🕑 11:30am-2:30pm Fri-Sun, 5:30-10:30pm daily, 11pm-4am Thu-Mon; 🚌 Ace Gold
If you're not feeling flush enough for chef Alessandro Stratta's high-end dining room (left), try his laid-back trattoria instead, with tables near the casino floor. Wood-oven-

fired pizzas, meatball sandwiches and pasta puttanesca keep both the pretheater and preclubbing crowds happy. Tiramisu, cannoli, bombolini and house-made sorbet and gelato tip the dessert scales.

SWITCH

Steakhouse $$

☎ 248-3463; Encore, 3131 Las Vegas Blvd S; ⏲ 5:30-10pm; 🚌 Deuce

Oh, how Vegas loves a gimmick! Here the atmosphere and indeed the entire interior design dramatically change every 20 minutes: walls slide back to reveal paintings, chandeliers drop and even the ambient music changes pace. In comparison, the straight-up steakhouse menu can be a yawn. Reservations recommended.

TABLEAU

Modern American $$

☎ 248-3463; www.wynnlasvegas.com; Tower Suites, Wynn, 3131 Las Vegas S; ⏲ 8-10:30am & 11:30am-2:30pm Mon-Fri, 8am-2:30pm Sat & Sun; 🚌 Ace Gold

Feel like a VIP inside Wynn's ivory Tower Suites. The biggest payoff at Tableau is at breakfast and brunch, which feature everything from watermelon juice and lemon-ricotta pancakes to tender Kobe beef sandwiches. Skip lunch, though (as it's not great value).

TERRACE POINT CAFÉ

American $$

☎ 248-3463; www.wynnlasvegas.com; Wynn, 3131 Las Vegas Blvd S; ⏲ 7am-10pm; 🚌 Ace Gold

A refined country-club atmosphere and sunny poolside patio take the casino coffee-shop concept to a whole new level. Well-rehearsed service, enormous portions and whopping prices are sure to knock you out.

DOWNTOWN

ALOHA SPECIALTIES

Fast Food $

☎ 385-1222; www.thecal.com; California, 12 E Ogden Ave; ⏲ 9am-9pm Sun-Thu, 9am-10pm Fri & Sat; 🚌 Deuce

Got-lucky gamblers and multi-generational families from Hawaii gather upstairs near the Cal's skybridge for true island tastes, like heaping plates of *kalua* pork or chicken *katsu* and bowls of saimin noodle soup. Lappert's Hawaiian ice cream parlor is nearby.

BINION'S CAFE

American $

☎ 382-1600; www.binions.com; Binion's, 128 E Fremont St; ⏲ 24hr, closed 7-10am Fri-Sun; 🚌 Deuce

On the main casino floor, this snack bar's old-fashioned counter plies fresh, never-frozen beef burgers piled high with crackling onions, iceberg lettuce and huge tomato slices. Chat with the sassy old-timers working the grill while wolfing down a slice of cherry pie.

BINION'S RANCH STEAKHOUSE
Steakhouse $$

☎ 382-1600; www.binions.com; Binion's, 128 E Fremont St; ⏰ 5-10:30pm; 🚌 Deuce

When high-rollin' cowboys finish up in the poker room, they tip back their Stetsons and ride the glass elevator up to this Old Vegas penthouse meatery for stunning 24th-floor views and

fine feasts of juicy chops with old-school fixins. Reservations recommended.

CHART HOUSE
Seafood $$

☎ 386-8364; www.chart-house.com; Golden Nugget, 129 E Fremont St; ⏰ 11:30am-11pm Mon-Thu, 11:30am-11:30pm Fri & Sat, 11:30am-10:30pm Sun; 🚌 Ace Gold

Perch on a barstool and let yourself be mesmerized by the 75,000-gallon tropical fish aquarium that's the centerpiece of this splashy seafood restaurant. The stuffed flounder, spiced yellowfin, macadamia-crusted mahi, crunchy coconut shrimp and

You may think you're eating in Italy at Grotto (p120)

seasonal stone crab claws on your plate are the real stars, though. Knock-out appetizers include a kimchi-flavored seafood martini and a zingy hummus trio.

🍴 DU-PAR'S
American/Seafood $

☎ 385-1906; www.goldengatecasino.net; Golden Gate, 1 E Fremont St; ⏱ 24hr, shrimp bar & deli 11am-3am; 🚌 Deuce Fluffy pancake breakfasts, old-fashioned blue-plate specials and fresh-baked donuts and pies are the attractions at this quaint diner inside Fremont St's most historic hotel (since 1906). At the San Francisco Shrimp Bar & Deli, order the best $1.99 shrimp cocktail in town (supersize it for two bucks more).

🍴 FLORIDA CAFÉ
Cuban $

☎ 385-3013; www.floridacafecuban.com; Howard Johnson hotel, 1401 Las Vegas Blvd S; ⏱ 8am-10pm; 🚌 Deuce; ♿
A hub for Naked City's Cuban community, the Florida has island artworks hanging on the walls and a Cuban chef reigning over the kitchen, cooking up shredded steak, hearty fried pork and seasoned chicken with yellow rice. *Café con leche,* flan and *batidos* (tropical shakes) are super.

🍴 GROTTO
Italian $$

☎ 385-7111; www.goldennugget.com; Golden Nugget, 129 E Fremont St; ⏱ 11:30am-10:30pm Sun-Thu, 11:30am-11:30pm Fri & Sat, pizza bar to midnight Sun-Thu, to 1am Fri & Sat; 🚌 Deuce Let yourself be drawn to the sunny patio beside the Nugget's shark-tank water slide and swimming pool. Gnocchi and osso bucco are the tenor of the old-world menu, but wood-oven-fired pizzas and a 200-bottle list of Italian wines are the real stars.

🍴 LUV-IT FROZEN CUSTARD
Takeout $

☎ 384-6452; www.luvitfrozencustard.com; 505 E Oakey Blvd; ⏱ 1-10pm Tue-Thu, 1-11pm Fri & Sat, also 1-10pm Sun & Mon May-Aug, closed Dec; 🚌 Deuce; Open since 1973, Luv-It offers handmade custard concoctions that are creamier than ice cream. Flavors change daily, so you'll be tempted to go back again, and again. Try a chocolate-dipped 'Luv Stick' bar, double-thick milkshake or superhero-sized sundae. Cash only.

🍴 MERMAIDS
Fast Food $

☎ 382-5777; 32 E Fremont St; ⏱ 24hr; 🚌 Deuce
Hook a strand of Mardi Gras beads at the door, then weave

your way past the bleary-eyed slot jockeys to belly up at the back counter for outrageous deep-fried Twinkies and Oreos snowed under by powdered sugar. So sinfully tasty.

🍴 TRIPLE GEORGE GRILL
Steakhouse/Seafood $$
☎ 384-2761; www.triplegeorgegrill.com; 201 N 3rd St; 🕑 11am-4pm Mon, 11am-10pm Tue-Fri, 4-10pm Sat; 🚍 Deuce
Showing off swank old-school San Francisco style, this hideaway is a haunt of the city's movers and shakers, attracted not only by its dry-aged steaks and classic seafood dishes, but also by its Rat Pack–worthy cocktails and rare wines, which are also poured next door at sidebar.

🍴 VIC & ANTHONY'S
Steakhouse/Seafood $$
☎ 386-8399; www.vicandanthonys .com; Golden Nugget, 129 E Fremont St; 🕑 5-11pm; 🚍 Deuce

---

BEST NOSHES OUTSIDE CASINOS
> Firefly (p122; also at the Plaza, p67)
> Hash House A Go Go (p126; also at the Imperial Palace, p66)
> Luv-It Frozen Custard (opposite)
> Origin India (p123)
> Rosemary's (p128)

Heavy red curtains, a faux stained-glass ceiling and high-backed leather chairs complement the serious atmosphere. The steakhouse menu covers the classics: jumbo lump crab cakes, Maine lobster, grain-fed Midwestern beef, Beluga caviar and a divine chocolate fudge cake. Reservations are recommended.

EAST OF THE STRIP

🍴 AGO
Italian $$
☎ 693-4440; www.hardrockhotel.com; Hard Rock, 4455 Paradise Rd; 🕑 6-11pm Sun-Thu, 6pm-midnight Fri & Sat; 🚍 108
Backed by Hollywood celeb Robert DeNiro, chef Agostino Sciandri's sleek eatery will be hard-pressed to fail. The elegant menu of northern Italian cuisine includes signature house-made pastas, thin-crust pizzas, wild-mushroom risotto, delicately done seafood and other meatier fare. Inspired desserts.

🍴 ENVY
Steakhouse $$
☎ 784-5716; www.envysteakhouse .com; Renaissance, 3400 Paradise Rd; 🕑 6:30am-2:30pm Mon-Sat, 6:30am-3pm Sun, 5-10pm daily; Ⓜ Convention Center
Envy's name is no lie. Near the convention center, powerbrokers recline against high-backed chairs

Settle back with a sangria at sizzling Firefly

amid a boldly splashed color palette. Both steaks and seafood get high marks, along with a smart wine list and inventive side dishes like bourbon creamed corn. At breakfast, early risers see the likes of lemony brioche French toast or gingerbread waffles topped with cinnamon gelato. Reservations recommended.

🍴 FIREFLY
Tapas $$

☎ 369-3971; www.fireflylv.com; Citibank Plaza, 3900 Paradise Rd; 🕙 11:30am-2am Sun-Thu, 11:30am-3am Fri & Sat; 🚌 108

Firefly is always packed with a fashionable local crowd, not just for the singles' scene on the late-night patio, but also for the food. Tapas-style dishes are often fusion-spiced, but still shake hands with Spanish tradition,

from *patatas bravas* to chorizo clams and vegetarian delights. A backlit bar dispenses the house specialty sangria and infused mojitos. On some nights, hot Latin turntablists spin. Reservations strongly recommended.

🍴 LINDO MICHOACAN
Mexican $$

☎ 735-6828; www.lindomichoacan. com; 2655 E Desert Inn Rd; 🕙 10:30am-11pm Mon-Thu, 10:30am-midnight Fri, 9am-midnight Sat, 9am-11pm Sun; 🚌 free Strip shuttle; 🚻

Handmade ceramics and faux adobe walls make this hideout feel far away from the Strip. Family recipes fill the gigantic and satisfy-ing menu of Mexican classics, including ranch-style seafood, chipotle *lengua* (beef tongue), chicken *molé* and *menudo* (tripe and hominy soup).

▥ LOTUS OF SIAM
Thai $$

☎ 735-3033; www.saipinchutima.com; 953 E Sahara Ave; ⏲ 11:30am-2pm Mon-Fri, 5:30-9:30pm Mon-Thu, 5:30-10pm Fri-Sun; 🚌 204; Ⓥ ♿

Saipin Chutima's authentic Northern Thai cooking has won almost as many awards as her distinguished European and New World wine cellar. This strip-mall hole-in-the-wall may not look like much, but foodies flock here.

▥ METRO PIZZA
Pizza $

☎ 736-1955; www.metropizza.com; 1395 E Tropicana Ave; ⏲ 11am-10pm Sun-Thu, 11am-11pm Fri & Sat; 🚌 201; ♿

If you don't make it out here to taste Vegas' best thin-crust pie, you can devour a cheesy slice at Metro's outpost in the 24-hour **Ellis Island Casino & Brewery** (☎ 312-5888; 4178 Koval Lane), east of the Strip.

▥ NOBU
Japanese Fusion $$$

☎ 693-5090; www.hardrockhotel.com; Hard Rock, 4455 Paradise Rd; ⏲ 6-11pm; 🚌 108

Iron Chef Matasuhisa's sequel to his NYC namesake is almost as good as the original. The beats are down-tempo, the setting pure Zen, with bamboo stalks sprouting up around the kitchen. Stick to Nobu's classics, such as

black cod with miso. Feeling flush? Try the chef's special *omakase* dinner (from $100). Reservations essential.

▥ ORIGIN INDIA
Indian $$

☎ 734-6342; www.originindia restaurant.com; 4480 Paradise Rd; ⏲ 11:30am-11:30pm; 🚌 108; Ⓥ

In a chic dining room flecked with gold and outfitted with high-backed leather chairs, an epic New World and European wine list is only a bonus. What reels in adventurous feasters is the imaginative Indian menu, ranging across the subcontinent from centuries-old royal recipes to modern fusion dishes. The tandoori grills are exceptional. Vegetarians might feel like they've reached nirvana.

▥ PAYMON'S MEDITERRANEAN CAFÉ
Mediterranean $$

☎ 731-6030; www.paymons.com; 4147 S Maryland Parkway; ⏲ 11am-1am; 🚌 109, 202, Ace C-Line; Ⓥ

A find for vegetarian-friendly Middle Eastern specialties such as baked eggplant with fresh garlic, baba ganoush, *bourrani* and hummus. Carnivores will savor the succulent rotisserie lamb, baked *kibbe* platter and the hot gyros and kebab sandwiches. The

John Curtas
Radio & TV restaurant critic, lawyer and insatiable food blogger (www. eatinglv.com)

How did you become a foodie? I read a lot and took cooking classes, including from Julia Child – I was the only guy in a room full of middle-aged women, taking notes and having fun. **When did Vegas get on the foodie map?** When 'French connection' chefs like Joël Robuchon (p108) and Guy Savoy (p104) showed up, that legitimized Vegas as a restaurant town. **What do people not know about food in Vegas?** Chefs' restaurants here can be just as good as the originals in NYC or Paris. **Biggest dining mistake tourists make?** Don't listen to concierges or cab drivers. **Is it worth eating off-Strip?** You're either a fool or a high roller if you eat Asian food in casino hotels. It's the same food as you'll get on Spring Mountain Rd (opposite) for double the price. **Best foodie event?** Vegas Uncork'd (www.vegasuncorked. com). You can walk up and just start talking to big-name chefs like Alaine Ducasse. You can't do that in South Beach.

next-door Hookah Lounge (p136) is seductive.

🍴 STUDIO B BUFFET
Buffet $$

☎ 797-1000; www.themresort.com; M Resort, 12300 Las Vegas Blvd S; 🕙 11am-9pm Mon-Fri, 10am-10pm Sat & Sun

Boasting a live-action TV cooking show studio, this is Vegas' tastiest off-Strip buffet. Fall in love with the gelato bar and all-you-can-eat seafood extravaganzas on weekends. Complimentary beer and wine.

WEST OF THE STRIP

🍴 ALIZÉ
French $$$

☎ 951-7000; www.alizelv.com; 56th fl, Palms, 4321 W Flamingo Rd; 🕙 5:30-10pm; 🚌 202

Las Vegas chef André Rochat's top-drawer gourmet room is named after a gentle Mediterranean trade wind. Enjoyed by nearly every table, the panoramic floor-to-ceiling views of the glittering Strip are even more stunning than the haute French cuisine. A wine-bottle tower dominates the room. Reservations here are essential. Dress to the nines.

🍴 CARNIVAL WORLD & VILLAGE SEAFOOD BUFFETS
Buffet $$

☎ 777-7777; www.riolasvegas.com; Rio, 3700 W Flamingo Rd; 🕙 Carnival World 8am-10pm, Village Seafood 4-10pm Sun-Thu, 3:30-10:30pm Fri & Sat; 🚌 free Strip shuttle

Some say Carnival World is Vegas' best all-around buffet, with wok-fried dishes, taco bars, fresh seafood and handmade gelato. Pricier Village Seafood is for those who can't get enough snow crab legs, lobster tails and fresh-shucked oysters, plus salads and house-made breads.

🍴 CHINATOWN PLAZA
Pan-Asian $

☎ 221-8448; www.lvchinatown.com; 4255 Spring Mountain Rd; 🕙 daily, hours vary; 🚌 203

Lively Asian restaurants anchor around the Chinese gate on Spring Mountain Rd in Chinatown, where you'll also find plenty of Hong Kong barbecue houses, Vietnamese pho shops, Japanese sushi bars and pan-Asian bubble-tea dispensaries.

🍴 GARDUÑO'S
Southwestern $$

☎ 942-7777; www.palms.com; Palms, 4321 W Flamingo Rd; 🕙 11am-3pm & 4-10pm; 🚌 202

From Albuquerque's famed restaurant, the *tradicional* menu of New Mexican fare features such authentic tastes as handmade pork tamales and blue-corn enchiladas filled with chicken and cheese and doused with green and red chili sauces. Belly up to the Blue Agave oyster and chili bar for shooters and coconut margaritas.

🍽 GOLDEN STEER
Steakhouse $$

☎ 384-4470; http://golden.snapsweb.com; 308 W Sahara Ave; ⏲ 11:30am-4:30pm Mon-Fri, 5-11pm daily; 🚌 Ace Gold

It's not the best steak in town. So why are you eating at this fabulously retro steakhouse with the steer's head out front? It's the same place where the Rat Pack and Elvis once dined. You're here to soak up the Old Vegas vibes.

🍽 HASH HOUSE A GO GO
American $$

☎ 804-4646; www.hashhouseagogo.com; 6800 W Sahara Ave, east of S Rainbow Blvd; ⏲ 7:30am-2:30pm daily, 5:30-9pm Mon-Thu, 5:30-10pm Fri & Sat; 🚌 204; V 👤

Before heading to Red Rock Canyon (p160), fill up on this So-Cal import's famed 'twisted farm food,' which has to be seen to be believed. The pancakes are as big as tractor tires and the farm-egg scrambles and huge hashes could knock over a cow. Meatloaf, pot

---

> ## BEST BREAKFAST BETS
> > Hash House A Go Go (left)
> > Le Village Buffet (Paris Las Vegas; p113)
> > Payard Bistro (Caesars Palace; p103)
> > Peppermill coffee shop (Fireside Lounge; p134)
> > Terrace Point Café (Wynn; p118)

pies, chicken 'n' biscuits and wild-boar sloppy joes are what's for dinner.

🍽 IN-N-OUT BURGER
Fast Food $

☎ 800-786-1000; www.in-n-out.com; 4888 Dean Martin Dr; ⏲ 10:30am-1am Sun-Thu, 10:30am-1:30am Fri & Sat; 🚌 201; 👤

At California's famous In-N-Out, where the beef patties are never frozen and the potatoes are hand-diced daily, there's a secret menu. Ask for your burger 'animal style' (with mustard, an onion-grilled bun and extra-special sauce).

🍽 LBS BURGER JOINT
American $

☎ 835-9393; www.redrocklasvegas.com; Red Rock, 11011 W Charleston Blvd; ⏲ 11:30am-10pm Sun-Thu, 11:30am-11pm Fri & Sat; 🚌 206; 👤

It's a detour from the Strip, but so worth the trip for all-natural, hand-crafted beef, turkey or veggie patties lovingly laid on house-made buns, and piled high with boundary-breaking toppings like brie and wild mushrooms or smoked bacon with a fried egg. With warm sourdough pretzel sticks plus a vodka milkshake, it all equals a happy meal for adults.

☶ N9NE
Steakhouse/Seafood $$$

☎ 933-9900; www.n9nesteakhouse .com; Palms, 4321 W Flamingo Rd; ☾ 5-10pm Sun-Thu, 5-11pm Fri & Sat; ☒ 202

The Palms' sizzling steakhouse is a fave spot to sometimes spy on Hollywood celebs. A dramatically lit room centers on the champagne caviar bar, while at tables and booths the Chicago-style aged steaks and chops keep on coming, along with everything else from oysters Rockefeller to Pacific-caught sashimi. Reservations essential.

☶ NOVE ITALIANO
Italian $$

☎ 942-6800; www.n9negroup.com; 51st fl, Palms, 4321 W Flamingo Rd; ☾ 5:30-10:30pm Sun-Thu, 5:30-11pm Fri & Sat; ☒ 202

Sittin' pretty, this postmod Italian charmer attracts the preclubbing set with its rococo furnishings and floor-to-ceiling neon-light views. Just like the decor, the menu is

simultaneously classic (pizzas, pastas, salads) and globally minded (yellowtail crudo).

☶ OYSTER BAR
Seafood/Southern $$

☎ 367-2411; www.palacestation.com; 2411 W Sahara Ave; ☾ 11am-11pm Sun-Thu, 11am-1am Fri & Sat; ☒ 204

You might have to queue for a seat at this little ol' seafood shack, incongruously situated in the middle of a busy locals' casino floor. But you'll know it was worth the wait once you taste the Cajun seafood gumbo and étouffée, steamed mussels and clams or San Francisco cioppino stew. Key-lime torte and NYC-style cheesecake are such sweet endings. No reservations.

☶ PING PANG PONG
Chinese $$

☎ 367-7111; www.goldcoastcasino .com; Gold Coast, 4000 W Flamingo Rd; ☾ 10am-3pm & 5pm-3am; ☒ 202

Asian tourists vote with their feet, and it's always crowded here. Designed by chef Kevin Wu, a wok-tossed menu ranges across the regions of China, from Beijing seafood stew to Shanghai noodles. At lunchtime the dim sum cart rolls around. Service is fast and furious at the less-expensive **Noodle Exchange** (☾ noon-11pm).

🍴 RAKU

Japanese $$

☎ 367-3511; www.raku-grill.com; 5030 Spring Mountain Rd; 🕑 6pm-3am Mon-Sat; 🚌 203

On the outskirts of Chinatown, this Japanese *robata*-style charcoal grill is a tasty journey. Take flight on an imported sake sampler, then dig into creative hot and cold appetizers, salty yakitori skewers, steaming bowls of udon noodle soup or *oden* snacks boiled in broth. There are only a handful of tables at this sleek spot, so make reservations or expect to wait outside for an hour or more.

🍴 ROSEMARY'S

Modern American $$

☎ 869-2251; www.rosemarysrestaurant .com; 8125 W Sahara Ave, west of S Buffalo Dr; 🕑 11:30am-2pm Mon-Fri, 5:30-10pm daily; 🚌 204

Words almost fail to describe the epicurean ecstasy you'll encounter here. Yes, it's in a strip mall, and it's a long drive from the Strip. But once you bite into such divine offerings as Texas barbecue shrimp with Maytag blue-cheese slaw or grilled pork chops with Creole mustard sauce, you'll forget about all that. Wine and beer pairings are sublime. Reservations essential.

Hang around for a drink at SushiSamba (p112)

🍴 SIMON
Modern American $$

☎ 944-3292; www.simonatpalmsplace. com; Palms Place, 4381 W Flamingo Rd; ⏰ 7am-11pm; 🚌 202

A hip crowds turns up at celebrity chef Kerry Simon's poolside kitchen. Most meals are hit-and-miss, but the Sunday brunch buffet can't be beat for haute comfort-food magic, from fried chicken and waffles to rice-krispie treats.

🍴 VEGGIE DELIGHT
Vegetarian $

☎ 310-6565; 3504 Wynn Rd; ⏰ 11am-9pm; 🚌 203; Ⓥ

South of Chinatown's main drag, this peaceful, Buddhist-owned vegetarian (and vegan, on request) restaurant offers Vietnamese-style soups, crispy baguette sandwiches and summer rolls. A healthy menu of Chinese herbal tonics is matched to your chakras.

🍴 VINTNER GRILL
Mediterranean $$

☎ 214-5590; www.vglasvegas.com; 10100 W Charleston Blvd, off Indigo Dr; ⏰ 11am-10pm Mon-Thu, 11am-11pm Fri, 4-11pm Sat & Sun

Inside an office park, this surprisingly elegant space lures romantics to its enchanting canopied patio, where white lights twinkle over white sofas. Bite into wood-oven-fired flatbreads, panini, seafood and soups at lunch. At dinner, classics such as veal London broil and lamb osso bucco show off continental touches. Decadent desserts are by Vosges Haut-Chocolat. Reservations are recommended here.

PLAY

The Strip is the obvious all-hours hot spot. Catch a stage show before midnight, groove to a DJ till dawn, then unwind at a sultry spa after noon. This cow town also attracts more than its share of headliners, including celebrity entertainers you may have thought were already dead – whoops!

You can go broke seeing and doing all there is to see and do on the Strip, or be entertained for zero money at fun, free-for-all spectacles like the Bellagio's dancing fountains. Las Vegans let loose at hipster haunts on the edges of downtown, student- and gay-friendly hangouts east of the Strip, strip clubs in industrial areas west of I-15, and neighborhood bars and casinos in the 'burbs.

Free alternative tabloids *Las Vegas Weekly* (www.lasvegasweekly.com) and *Las Vegas CityLife* (www.lvcitylife.com) hit the streets on Thursday and, when combined with the 'Neon' section of the *Las Vegas Review-Journal* on Friday, offer comprehensive arts, entertainment and events listings. So do free, encyclopedic tourist mags such as *What's On, Las Vegas Magazine* and *Showbiz Weekly*.

THAT'S THE TICKET!

Ticketmaster (☎ 800-745-3000; www.ticketmaster.com) Tickets for major sporting events, headliner concerts and more.

Tix 4 Tonight (☎ 877-849-4868; www.tix4tonight.com; ⏰ most branches 10am-8pm) Center Strip (Bill's Gamblin' Hall & Saloon, p64; Casino Royale, p65; Fashion Show, p92); downtown (Four Queens, 202 E Fremont St); North Strip (south of the Riviera, 2955 Las Vegas Blvd S); South Strip (Hawaiian Marketplace, 3743 Las Vegas Blvd S; Showcase Mall, 3785 Las Vegas Blvd S) Same-day discount tickets for shows, attractions and tours.

Top left Lose your Zen on the dance floor at Tao (p144) **Bottom left** Dazzle and be dazzled on the patio of Pure (p143)

LAS VEGAS

PLAY

LAS VEGAS CALENDAR

Las Vegas is a nonstop party 24/7/365. Holidays (p192) are taken to the max, with New Year's Eve along the Strip seeing the biggest crush of humanity this side of Times Sq. Major sports events (p149) also pack the city like a full house. Contact the **Las Vegas Convention & Visitors Authority** (LVCVA; ☎ 892-0711, 877-847-4858; www.visitlasvegas.com; 3150 Paradise Rd; ⏱ office 8am-5pm, toll-free hotline 7am-7pm) for current events info.

February/March

Vegas High Rollers (www.lvscooterrally.com) Retro live bands and dances, *Gong Show* karaoke nights, poker tournaments and fab happy hours jazz up this scooter rally.

April

UNLVino (www.unlvino.com) Nonprofit wine-tasting extravaganza brings together oenophiles to taste more than 750 vintages, plus a celebrity wine auction.

Viva Las Vegas (www.vivalasvegas.net) Ultimate rockabilly weekend comes alive with a tiki pool party, jive-dancing classes, a va-va-va-voom burlesque competition and a souped-up classic car show.

May

Helldorado Days (www.elkshelldorado.com) Dating back to the 1930s, this historic hoedown features rodeo events, trail rides, country-and-western bands and DJs, a family-friendly carnival, a parade and fireworks downtown.

June & July

CineVegas (www.cinevegas.com) Temporarily on hiatus, this prestigious film festival showcases indie flicks, first-time directors and Hollywood stars at Brenden Theatres (p137).

BARS

Most of Sin City's watering holes are smoke-filled; limited smoking bans apply at bars serving food (see p183). Many bars stay open until 2am or even around the clock. Happy hours are usually 4pm till 7pm, with 'graveyard' happy hours around midnight.

107 LOUNGE

☎ 380-7711; www.topoftheworldlv .com; 107th fl, Stratosphere Tower, 2000 Las Vegas Blvd S; elevator ride $16; ⏱ 4pm-1am Sun-Thu, 4pm-2am Fri & Sat; Ⓜ Sahara

There's no place to get any higher in Vegas without the approval of an air-traffic controller. From Wednesday through Saturday

World Series of Poker (www.wsop.com) High-stakes gamblers, casino employees and celebrities match wits in over 40 tournaments. Free public viewing.

August
Def Con (www.defcon.org) The nation's biggest conclave of underground computer hackers takes place over a long, heavily caffeinated weekend.

September
Las Vegas BikeFest (www.lasvegasbikefest.com) This bike rally brings hogs and heifers and Harley-riding poker players roaring into town, with custom-bike shows and bikinis part of the debauchery.

October
Professional Bull Riders World Finals (www.pbrnow.com) Happening over five days in mid-October, PBR brings real-life buckin' bronco action to town.

November
Aviation Nation (www.nellis.af.mil) At Nellis Air Force Base, this is the nation's most famous military and civilian air show, during which the Thunderbirds, an aerial demonstration team, often zoom in.

December
Wrangler National Finals Rodeo (www.nfrexperience.com) This hugely popular 10-day event features professional rodeo cowboys competing in a half-dozen adrenaline-driven events, including steer wrestling and bull riding.

evenings, smooth jazz accompanies the 'elevated' martinis swilled by a moneyed crowd of cocktail-hour couples. Chic dress code.

⭐ **BAR AT TIMES SQUARE**
☎ 740-6466; www.nynyhotelcasino .com; Greenwich Village, New York–New York, 3790 Las Vegas Blvd S; cover $10, reserved seat $15 Sun-Thu, $25 Fri & Sat; ⏲ 24hr (live music 8pm-2am); Ⓜ MGM Grand

Baby boomers will dig the sing-along vibe at this dueling piano bar. Show up early or risk waiting outside in Greenwich Village, where latecomers strain to catch a glimpse of the drunken festivities inside.

⭐ BEAUTY BAR
☎ 598-1965; www.beautybar.com; 517 E Fremont St; cover free-$10; ☽ usually 10pm-4am; 🚌 Ace Gold

Swill a cocktail, watch the weekly manicure demonstrations or just chill inside the salvaged innards of a 1950s New Jersey beauty salon. DJs and live bands rotate nightly here, spinning tiki lounge tones, '80s garage rock, punk, funk and soul. Make sure you wear your coolest vintage threads.

⭐ CARNAVAL COURT
☎ 369-5000; www.harrahslasvegas .com; outside Harrah's, 3475 Las Vegas Blvd S; cover free-$10; ☽ noon-2am Sun-Thu, noon-3am Fri & Sat; Ⓜ Harrah's/Imperial Palace

Flair bartenders juggle fire for raucous crowds for whom spring break never ended. Live pop and rock cover bands tear up the stage at night, but all eyes are on the hot bods at the bar. Party on, dudes.

⭐ DOWNTOWN COCKTAIL ROOM
☎ 880-3696; www.downtownlv.net; 111 Las Vegas Blvd S; cover free-$10; ☽ 4pm-2am Mon-Fri, 7pm-2am Sat; 🚌 Ace Gold

With a retro cocktail list you must take seriously, this speakeasy with sateen pillows and suede-covered couches feels decades removed from the old-school carpet joints on Fremont St. In

DRINKS WITH VIP VIEWS
> 107 Lounge (Stratosphere; p132)
> Foundation Room (Mandalay Bay; p142)
> ghostbar (Palms; p153)
> Mandarin Bar & Tea Lounge (City-Center; p136)
> Mix (THEhotel at Mandalay Bay; p137)

true Prohibition-era style, the entrance is disguised.

⭐ FIRESIDE LOUNGE
☎ 735-4177; www.peppermilllasvegas .com; Peppermill, 2985 Las Vegas Blvd S; ☽ 24hr; 🚌 Deuce

Don't be blinded by the outlandish rainbow-colored neon lights: the Strip's most spellbinding hideaway (p18) awaits inside this retro coffee shop. Courting couples adore the sunken fire pit, cozy blue-velvet nooks and faux tropical foliage. Sip a Scorpion.

⭐ FRANKIE'S TIKI ROOM
☎ 385-3110; www.frankiestikiroom. com; 1712 W Charleston Blvd; ☽ 24hr; 🚌 206

West of I-15 and downtown's 18b Arts District, this genuine tiki bar (see p141) with kitschy tropical decor is a locals' hideout. Libations are rated by potency from one to five skulls (watch out for the Zombie and Green Gasser!).

⭐ FREEZONE

☎ 794-2300; www.freezonelv.com; 610 E Naples Dr, off Paradise Rd; ⏲ 24hr; 🚍 108

Every night is a party at this gay dive bar. Tuesday is ladies' night with go-go girls, Thursday is boyz' night with go-go boys, Friday and Saturday nights feature the 'Queens of Las Vegas' drag cabaret, and Sunday and Monday are for free pool and no-wait karaoke.

⭐ GILLEY'S

☎ 894-7111; www.gilleyslasvegas.com; TI (Treasure Island), 3300 Las Vegas Blvd S; ⏲ 11am-2am Sun-Thu, 11am-4am Fri & Sat; 🚍 Deuce

Yee-haw! Bring on the line-dancing cowboys and bikini-clad mechanical-bull-riding cowgirls at this country-and-western theme bar, dance hall (live bands or DJs) and Southern barbecue joint.

⭐ GRIFFIN

☎ 382-0577; 511 E Fremont St; ⏲ 5pm-2am Mon-Sat, 9pm-2am Sun; 🚍 Deuce

Escape from the casinos' clutch and imbibe at this indie joint, a short walk along the dark side of Fremont St. Crackling fireplaces, leather booths and an almost unbearably cool jukebox make it popular with hipster sweethearts and rebels alike.

Choose your own wicked concoction at Carnaval Court

SPECIALTY DRINKS

Hostile Grape (M Resort; ☎ 797-1000, 12300 Las Vegas Blvd S) A robust global wine list is poured from the self-dispensing system in the casino's cellar.

Isla Tequila Bar (Isla Mexican Kitchen; p115) Taste a wonderland of premium agave elixirs. For sultry surroundings, drop by **Dos Caminos** (Palazzo; p111).

Laguna Champagne Bar (Palazzo; p54) A circular cocktail lounge in the midst of the Palazzo's busy casino floor serves 'boom boom' shooters, deluxe champagne cocktails and premium labels of bubbly by the glass or bottle.

Nine Fine Irishmen (New York–New York; p53) Stout Irish beers, rare whiskies and other spirits; traditional music and Celtic rock; and Brooklyn Bridge views.

Pour 24 (New York–New York; p53) Next to the pedestrian skybridge, North American microbrews on draft or in bottles are popped open around the clock.

⭐ HOFBRÄUHAUS

☎ 853-2337; www.hofbrauhauslas
vegas.com; 4510 Paradise Rd; ⏲ 11am-
11pm Sun-Thu, 11am-midnight Fri & Sat;
🚌 108

A fawning replica of the original in Munich, this $12-million beer hall and garden celebrates Oktoberfest all year with premium imported suds, big Bavarian pretzels, fair fräuleins, trademark *gemütlichkeit* (congeniality) and oom-pah-pah bands from Germany on weekends.

⭐ HOOKAH LOUNGE

☎ 731-6030; www.hookahlounge
.com; 4147 S Maryland Parkway;
⏲ 5pm-1am; 🚌 109, 202, Ace C-Line
Next to Paymon's Mediterranean Café (p123), you can recline languorously with a water pipe stuffed with one of 20 premium flavored Egyptian tobaccos. Exotic fig-

flavored cocktails are pricier than the off-Strip norm, but for ambience worthy of a pasha, why not?

⭐ MANDARIN BAR & TEA LOUNGE

☎ 590-8888; www.mandarinoriental.
com/lasvegas; Mandarin Oriental, 3752 Las Vegas Blvd S; ⏲ 10am-1am Sun-Thu, 10am-2am Fri & Sat; 🚌 Deuce
With panoramic Strip views from the hotel's 23rd-floor Sky Lobby, this sophisticated lounge serves exotic teas by day and champagne cocktails by night. Indulge in full afternoon tea service or spoonful-sized global-fusion appetizers after dark.

⭐ MINUS5 ICE LOUNGE

☎ 740-5800; www.minus5experience.
com; Mandalay Place, 3930 Las Vegas Blvd S; cover from $25, usually incl 1 drink; ⏲ 11am-3am; 🚌 Deuce

In a city known for over-the-top gimmicks, this bar has quite a reputation. Don borrowed coats and hats before stepping inside the tiny inner sanctum, kept at an arctic chilled -5°C (23°F), where everything is made of ice, from artistic sculptures to the glasses your cocktails are served in. Spoiler alert: no personal photo-taking allowed inside.

⭐ MIX

☎ 632-9500; www.mandalaybay.com; 64th fl, THEhotel at Mandalay Bay, 3950 Las Vegas Blvd S; cover after 10pm $20-25; ⏲ 5pm-2am Sun-Thu, 5pm-4am Fri & Sat; 🚌 Deuce

Arrive at around sunset for a free glass-elevator ride up to this sky-high restaurant lounge with some of Las Vegas' most breathtaking views – and that's even before you glimpse the wall-to-wall leather seating and the champagne bar. Go hobnobbing on the vertiginous outdoor patio.

⭐ RHUMBAR

☎ 792-7615; www.mirage.com; Mirage, 3400 Las Vegas Blvd S; ⏲ noon-midnight Sun-Thu, noon-2am Fri & Sat; Ⓜ Harrah's/Imperial Palace

Minty mojitos and frozen daiquiris are pure mixology magic at this Caribbean-flavored bar and cigar lounge. Rhumbar is handy

to the Mirage's south entrance. Chill at breezy, beachy open-air lounge tables on the chic Strip-view patio.

⭐ TRIPLE 7

☎ 387-1896; www.mainstreetcasino.com; Main Street Station, 200 N Main St; ⏲ 24hr; 🚌 Deuce

Sports fans and a crusty crowd of local gamblers flock to this gargantuan brewpub for *Monday Night Football*, happy hour and graveyard specials. Five microbrews on tap (including specialty fruit beers) and cheap pub grub sate the punters. Don't expect snappy service, though.

⭐ CINEMAS

Check **Fandango** (☎ 800-326-3264; www.fandango.com) for show times and tickets.

⭐ BRENDEN THEATRES & IMAX

☎ 507-4849; www.brendentheatres.com; Palms, 4321 W Flamingo Rd; adult/concession $11/7, IMAX $15/12; 🚌 202; ♿

Showing new Hollywood releases, as well as independent film-festival-circuit features and documentaries, the swankiest off-Strip movieplex is fitted with IMAX and Dolby 3D Digital Cinema, plus rocker-chair stadium seating for superior sight lines.

LAS VEGAS

PLAY

⭐ REGAL VILLAGE SQUARE 18

☎ 221-2283; 9400 W Sahara Ave at S Fort Apache Rd; adult/concession $11/7; 🚌 204; ♿

Las Vegas doesn't really have any arthouse cinemas, but this multiplex way out west of the Strip usually has a couple of interesting indie flicks up on the marquee.

⭐ WEST WIND LAS VEGAS 5 DRIVE-IN

☎ 646-3565; 4150 W Carey Ave, east of N Rancho Dr; adult/child $6.25/1; ☉ gates open 1hr before show time; ♿

One of Nevada's last remaining drive-ins, this old-fashioned place screens up to five double features daily. Bring your buddies, grab some popcorn and put your feet up on the dashboard – ah, heaven.

⭐ COMEDY & MAGIC

Big-name comedians frequently headline at Caesars Palace (p43), the Flamingo (p46), the Golden Nugget (p47), Mandalay Bay (see the boxed text, p151), the Mirage (p52), MGM Grand (see the boxed text, p151) and the Venetian (p62).

⭐ COMEDY STOP

☎ 737-2111; www.comedystop.com; Sahara, 2535 Las Vegas Blvd S; tickets $25-40; ☉ usually 9pm nightly; Ⓜ Sahara

Be sure to check out the A-list funny men and women cracking up the crowd at the Sahara. You can find them in the Congo Room at this Atlantic City export.

⭐ THE IMPROV

☎ 369-5223; www.improv.com; Harrah's, 3475 Las Vegas Blvd S; tickets $20-45; ☉ usually 8:30pm & 10:30pm Tue, Thu & Sat; Ⓜ Harrah's/Imperial Palace

The Vegas franchise of this NYC-based chain has that signature Big Apple brick backdrop. The spotlight is on many of the touring stand-up headliners of the moment, often polished by recent late-night TV appearances.

⭐ MAC KING

☎ 369-5222; www.mackingshow .com; Harrah's, 3475 Las Vegas Blvd S; tickets $25; ☉ 1pm & 3pm Tue-Sat; Ⓜ Harrah's/Imperial Palace; ♿

Redheaded Mac has the front-running afternoon magic and comedy show in town, with lots of PG-13 laughs and sleight-of-hand thrown in. He really rides the crazy train with his bag of tricks, which includes baiting a live goldfish with a Fig Newton cookie.

⭐ PENN & TELLER

☎ 777-7776; www.pennandteller.com; Rio, 3700 W Flamingo Rd; tickets $75-85; ☉ 9pm Sat-Thu; 🚌 free Strip shuttle

This intellectual odd couple (one talks, the other doesn't) has been creating and destroying illusions for over two decades, with dry wit, peppery profanity and some amazing stunts such as catching bullets in their teeth. The gimmick is that they actually explain some (but not all) of their tricks to the audience.

VINNIE FAVORITO

☎ 733-3333; www.flamingolasvegas.com; Flamingo, 3555 Las Vegas Blvd S; tickets $55-66; ⏱ usually 8pm nightly; Ⓜ Flamingo/Caesars Palace

Rude, crude and shockingly funny (his motto: 'Completely F'n Crazy!'), this stand-up comedian pulls no punches in Bugsy's Cabaret. No topic is off-limits, from rednecks to celebrities in rehab. Sit too close to the stage and you might be the butt of Favorito's next joke.

LIVE MUSIC

Touring headliners also sell out the city's megaconcert venues (see the boxed text, p151). For Vegas' famous Elvis impersonator tribute shows, surf to www.thedreamking.com.

BUNKHOUSE SALOON

☎ 384-4536; www.bunkhouselv.com; 124 S 11th St; ⏱ 24hr; 🚌 107

As you might have guessed, it's got a cowboy theme, with Old West art and saddles lying about.

LAS VEGAS IDOL

Dino's (☎ 382-3894; 1516 Las Vegas Blvd S; 🚌 Deuce) At this downtown dive bar favored by artists, hipsters and indie types, 'no bullshit' karaoke takes over on Thursday, Friday and Saturday nights (with Jägerbombs!).

Ellis Island (☎ 733-8901; 4178 Koval Lane; 🚌 202) Off-Strip casino dive with cheap microbrews and nightly karaoke from 9pm to 3am.

Harrah's Piano Bar (near Carnaval Court; p134) It's TJ's All-Star Karaoke Party before 9pm most nights, with plasma screens, impressionists and stand-up comedy acts.

Karaoke Club (Imperial Palace; p66) Choose from over 15,000 songs and have your performance immortalized on DVD any night of the week. If you're lucky, you'll perform even better than the IP's 'dealertainers' (p78).

But the real draws are live local bands, anything from rockabilly to rock to reggae, along with indie film and stand-up comedy nights.

CROWN THEATER

☎ 888-727-6966; http://thecrowntheater.com; Rio, 3700 W Flamingo Rd; tickets from $25; ⏱ hours vary; 🚌 free Strip shuttle

See your favorite tribute band or pop, rock, punk or country act live at this 900-seat theater-in-the-round, brought to you by the same brain trust behind LA's Viper

Room. Anyone from Devo to the Magnetic Zeros plays here.

★ DOUBLE DOWN SALOON

☎ 791-5775; www.doubledownsaloon.com; 4640 Paradise Rd, enter off Swenson St; ☽ 24hr; 🚌 108

You just gotta love a punk bar where the tangy, blood-red house drink is named 'Ass Juice.' There's never a cover charge, and the drinks (try the bacon martini) are cash only. Monday is the Bargain DJ Collective night, and there are lotsa lunatic-fringe bands other nights. Play pool, pinball, Asteroids or the legendary jukebox.

★ HOUSE OF BLUES

☎ 632-7600; www.hob.com; Mandalay Bay, 3950 Las Vegas Blvd S; most tickets $20-100; ☽ hours vary; 🚌 Deuce

Blues is the tip of the hog at this Mississippi Delta juke joint, where kickin' acts range from living legends to alt-rockers. Seating is limited, so show up early. Sight lines are good, and the tattoo studio is packed with twentysomethings.

★ THE JOINT BY ROGUE

☎ 693-5000; www.hardrockhotel.com; Hard Rock, 4455 Paradise Rd; most tickets $25-100; ☽ hours vary; 🚌 108

Concerts at this intimate venue feel like private shows, even when Coldplay or the Beastie Boys are in town. It's a beacon for rock 'n' roll

superstars. Most shows here are standing-room only, with reservable VIP balcony seats upstairs.

★ THE PEARL

☎ 944-3200; www.palmspearl.com; Palms, 4321 W Flamingo Rd; most tickets $45-150; ☽ hours vary; 🚌 202

A beacon for rock bands, the Palms' concert hall has a sophisticated sound system and on-site recording studio. Modern rock acts like Gwen Stefani and Morrissey have burned up the stage, with most seats only 120ft or less away from the stars.

★ SMOKIN' HOT ACES

☎ 541-8700; www.smokinhotaces.com; Venetian, 3355 Las Vegas Blvd S; ☽ 5pm-1am; Ⓜ Harrah's/Imperial Palace

Just outside the Grand Canal Shoppes, near the Venetian's faux Rialto Bridge, this hideaway gin joint mixes poker-themed decor with pure rock 'n' roll attitude and live bands. Play pool and drop quarters into the 11,000-song jukebox while your buds guzzle Pabst Blue Ribbon beer and knock-out, flaming-red, 48oz house cocktails.

★ NIGHTCLUBS

Ladies sometimes get in free before midnight, especially on weeknights. Call ahead for bottle-service reservations (minimum $350 per threesome, two-bottle minimum per table). Check *Las Vegas Weekly*

P Moss
Short-story writer, gambler & owner of Frankie's Tiki Room (p134)

Tell us about your customers. You might see 10 people sitting at the bar, and they're all different, from the guy with the suit to one with a mohawk. It's the kind of place that makes everyone happy. **What gave you the idea for a tiki bar?** Vegas actually has a tiki history, from Aku Aku at the Stardust to the Venetian's Taboo Cove. **What makes your bar one-of-a-kind?** It's traditional, but skewed with kitsch. The world's top tiki carvers, from Bamboo Ben to LeRoy Schmaltz, made original art for us. **Who's Frankie?** This bar has been around since the 1940s, which in Vegas makes it historic. I kept the name, to walk the fence between preservationists and progress. **What's the biggest misconception visitors have about Vegas?** People don't realize how much of a suburban strip-mall culture it is. That's why we need places like Frankie's, to be the exception to that rule – and every rule.

(www.lasvegasweekly.com) for club event calendars.

☆ THE BANK

☎ 693-8300; www.lightgroup.com; Bellagio, 3600 Las Vegas Blvd S; cover $30-50; ☽ 10:30pm-4am Thu-Sun; Ⓜ Bally's/Paris

A celeb hangout since the day it opened, the posh reincarnation of Light nightclub is cloaked in royal-purple curtains and chandeliers. Lavish multitiered VIP booths are layered around a glass-enclosed dance floor where high-NRG pop and hip-hop mixes dominate. Upscale dress code.

☆ FOUNDATION ROOM

☎ 632-7614; www.hob.com; 43rd fl, Mandalay Bay, 3950 Las Vegas Blvd S; ☽ 11pm-late; 🚌 Deuce

House of Blues' (p140) exclusive club atop M-Bay hosts after-show parties in a luxurious lounge with gothic and Indian-temple decor. Celebs such as Andre Agassi hold court, while DJs and special events like Monday's **Godspeed** (☎ 632-7631; www.myspace.com/godspeedlasvegas) enliven the vibe. Call in advance to get on the VIP guest list.

☆ JET

☎ 693-8300; www.lightgroup.com; Mirage, 3400 Las Vegas Blvd S; cover $20-40; ☽ 10:30pm-4am Thu-Sat & Mon; 🚌 Deuce

A sophisticated tri-environment club, Jet once broke the sound barrier in racing to the creamy top of the Strip's nightlife scene. Follow the flickering candles and a staircase made for strutting onto the throbbing dance floor, or sidle into more intimate lounges where the beats run to deep house and hip hop. Stylish attire required.

☆ KRÄVE

☎ 290-0436; www.kravelasvegas.com; Miracle Mile Shops, 3663 Las Vegas Blvd S, enter off Harmon Ave; cover $10-20; ☽ 11pm-late Tue-Sun; Ⓜ Bally's/Paris

The Strip's only gay club is a glam place packed wall-to-wall with hard bodies, plush booth seating, VIP cabanas and even 'airotic' flyboys. The side lounge has salsa, goth and Candybar girls-only nights. Saturday's after-hours party revs up after 4am.

☆ LAX

☎ 262-4529; www.laxthenightclub.com; Luxor, 3900 Las Vegas Blvd S; cover $20-40; ☽ 10pm-4am Wed, Fri & Sat; 🚌 Deuce

Strut your stuff inside this vaguely gothic nightclub. VIP tables border the dance floor that's like an airport runway between two giant bars. Nights hosted by Hollywood A-listers and socialites are pulse-pounding.

⭐ MOON

☎ 942-6832; www.n9negroup.com; 53rd fl, Fantasy Tower, Palms, 4321 W Flamingo Rd; cover $20-40; ⏰ 10pm-4am Tue & Thu-Sun; 🚌 202

A short glass-and-mirror elevator ride away from the **Playboy Club** (☎ 942-6832; 52nd fl, Fantasy Tower; cover $20-40, incl Moon nightclub; ⏰ 9pm-4am), this futuristic penthouse has a surreal moon roof that retracts as you find your groove in the laser-lit fog on the dance floor below. Glass tiles change color with the mood and beat of the music, whether DJs are spinning hip hop, rock or pop and retro mash-ups. Dress to impress.

⭐ PIRANHA

☎ 791-0100; www.piranhalasvegas. net; 4633 Paradise Rd; cover $10-20; ⏰ 10pm-late; 🚌 108

The gay universe of the Fruit Loop orbits Sin City's sexiest gay nightclub, decked out with fireplace patios, aquariums and waterfalls, plus the luxurious 8½ Ultra Lounge. Expect outrageous theme parties, drag cabarets, and ladies-only and Latin nights.

⭐ PURE

☎ 731-7873; www.purethenightclub .com; Caesars Palace, 3570 Las Vegas Blvd S; cover $20-40; ⏰ 10pm-4am Tue & Fri-Sun; Ⓜ Flamingo/Caesars Palace

With gorgeous female DJs, this chic modern club electrifies with

---

UNDER-THE-RADAR NIGHTSPOTS

> Beauty Bar (p134)
> Downtown Cocktail Room (p134)
> Drai's (p153)
> Fireside Lounge (p134)
> Foundation Room (opposite)

its hues of electric blue, white and silver. Crowds of fine young thangs lounge inside a labyrinth of rooms that feel a lot like LA, and which lead to a gorgeous Strip-view patio. Strict dress code.

⭐ RAIN

☎ 942-6832; www.n9negroup.com; Palms, 4321 W Flamingo Rd; cover $20-40; ⏰ 11pm-4am Fri & Sat; 🚌 202

Britney Spears once threw an impromptu concert while partying at this long-time survivor club. The bamboo dance floor appears to float on a layer of fountains, while fog and pyrotechnics set the partyin' mood. International jet-set DJ Paul Oakenfold currently spins here on many Saturday nights.

⭐ STONEY'S ROCKIN' COUNTRY

☎ 435-2855; www.stoneysrockin country.com; 9151 Las Vegas Blvd S; cover $10; ⏰ 7pm-late Thu-Sun; 🚌 117

Yee-haw! It's Vegas' biggest country-and-western dance hall and saloon, where a lustful crowd stares slack-jawed at the mechanical bull riding. With DJs or live music every weekend and a wide-open dance floor, it's a rowdy place to kick up your cowboy boots.

⭐ TAO

☎ 388-8588; www.taolasvegas.com; Grand Canal Shoppes, Venetian, 3355 Las Vegas Blvd S; cover $20-40; 🕙 10pm-5am Thu-Sat; Ⓜ Harrah's/Imperial Palace

Modeled after the Asian-themed NYC club, here svelte, nearly naked go-go girls covered only by strategically placed flowers splash in bathtubs while another in yogi garb assumes the lotus position on a pedestal high above the risqué dance floor, where Paris Hilton look-alikes forego enlightenment to bump-and-grind to earthy hip hop instead.

⭐ VANITY

☎ 693-4000; www.vanitylv.com; Hard Rock, 4455 Paradise Rd; cover $20-40; 🕙 10pm-4am Thu-Sun; 🚌 108

Stylin' like a rock star, this chic nightclub has famous faces hanging in VIP rooms, while hoi-polloi masses bump to hip-hop, house and rock tunes around the 'cyclone' crystal chandelier and on the onyx catwalk. Thursday's 'Godskitchen' and Sunday's 'Sin' are big nights here. Free beauty-salon touch-ups in the ladies' room (remember to tip).

⭐ XS

☎ 770-0097; www.xslasvegas.com; Encore, 3111 Las Vegas Blvd S; cover $20-40; 🕙 10pm-4am Fri-Mon; 🚌 Ace Gold

Snakeskin banquettes, ultrasuede sofas, a glittering chandelier and arty gold facades adorn this luxe club. Settle in with your all-hours entourage at a VIP cabana by the outdoor lagoon, where dancing divas kick off their heels and make a splash on hot summer nights. DJs are mostly mainstream. Dress to impress.

⭐ PRODUCTION SHOWS

The most in-demand tix are for Cirque du Soleil extravaganzas and straight-off-Broadway musicals. Old-school shows involve minimal plot with a variety of kitschy song, dance and magic numbers. A grab-bag of erotically themed shows, from rock musicals to late-night vampire revues, are rarely worth the money.

⭐ CÉLINE DION

☎ 731-7110, 877-423-5463; www.celineinvegas.com; Caesars Palace, 3570 Las Vegas Blvd S; tickets $55-250; 🕙 usually 7:30pm Tue, Wed & Fri-Sun; Ⓜ Flamingo/Caesars Palace

No one rules the Colosseum's stage like this French-Canadian chanteuse, although other divas such as Bette Midler, Cher and Elton John have tried to fill her glamorous shoes. In a brand-new Vegas spectacular, meant to be a tribute to the romance of Old Hollywood, Céline reprises her greatest hits accompanied by a live orchestra.

★ CRAZY HORSE PARIS

☎ 891-7777, 866-740-7711; www.mgmgrand.com; MGM Grand, 3799 Las Vegas Blvd S; tickets $47-57; ⏰ 8pm & 10:30pm Wed-Mon; Ⓜ MGM Grand
Za-za-zoom. At the artiest topless show in town, the 100% red room's intimate bordello feel oozes sex appeal. Onstage, balletic dancers straight from Paris' Crazy Horse Saloon perform cabaret numbers interspersed with voyeuristic and humorous *l'art du nu* vignettes and black-and-white film clips.

★ CRISS ANGEL: BELIEVE

☎ 262-4400, 800-557-7428; www.cirquedusoleil.com; Luxor, 3900 Las Vegas Blvd S; tickets $59-160; ⏰ 7pm & 9:30pm Tue-Sat; 🚍 Deuce
The peripatetic French-Canadian circus troupe Cirque du Soleil mixes high-adrenaline stunts, surreal postmodern fantasy and dark, dreamy magical illusions with pop-star illusionist Criss Angel, who stars as a Victorian lord beset by buxom beauties.

★ DIVAS LAS VEGAS

☎ 731-3311, 800-351-7400; www.imperialpalace.com; Imperial Palace, 3535 Las Vegas Blvd S; tickets $69-79; ⏰ 10pm Sat-Thu; Ⓜ Harrah's/Imperial Palace
In this mainstream female-impersonator revue, the award-winning Frank Marino (who had a cameo in *Miss Congeniality 2*) acts as a catty Joan Rivers, dispensing naughty jokes and remarks between mostly lip-synched impersonations of Diana Ross, Cher and Liza Minnelli.

★ JUBILEE!

☎ 967-4567, 800-237-7469; www.ballyslasvegas.com; Bally's, 3645 Las Vegas Blvd S; tickets $53-113; ⏰ 7:30pm & 10:30pm Sat-Thu; Ⓜ Bally's/Paris
Girls, girls, girls! It's a showgirl production that Vegas wouldn't be Vegas without. As it started, so does it end: with lots of knockers, twinkling rhinestones and enormous headdresses on display. If you can forgive the giant helping of cheese, it's a riot.

★ KÀ

☎ 796-9999, 877-264-1844; http://ka.com; MGM Grand, 3799 Las Vegas Blvd S; tickets adult $69-150, child $35-75; ⏰ 7pm & 9:30pm Tue-Sat; Ⓜ MGM Grand; ♿
Cirque du Soleil makes this sensuous but impossible-to-follow story of imperial twins, mysterious destinies, love and conflict a hot

PEEK BEHIND THE SHOWGIRLS' CURTAIN

Bally's **Backstage Tour** (☎ 946-4567, 800-237-7469) runs one-hour backstage tours of its long-running spectacular, Donn Arden's *Jubilee!* (p145). The tours ($15, with show-ticket purchase $10) offer a behind-the-scenes look at the hidden lives of Las Vegas showgirls and chorus boys, starting at 11am Monday, Wednesday and Saturday.

ticket. Instead of a stage, there's a grid of moving platforms for a frenzy of martial-arts-inspired performances. Premium seats hold court at the back.

⭐ LA RÊVE

☎ 770-9966, 888-320-7110; www.wynnlasvegas.com; Wynn, 3131 Las Vegas Blvd S; tickets $99-179; 🕑 7pm & 9:30pm Fri-Tue; 🚌 Deuce

Aquatic acrobatic feats by scuba-certified performers are the centerpiece of this theater, which holds a one-million-gallon swimming pool; critics call it a less-inspiring version of Cirque's *O*. Beware: the cheap seats are in the 'splash zone.' The VIP 'Indulgence' package offers champagne and chocolate-covered strawberries, as well as personal video monitors for close-ups of the performance and behind-the-scenes glimpses.

⭐ LEGENDS IN CONCERT

☎ 369-5111; www.legendsinconcert.com; Harrah's, 3475 Las Vegas Blvd S; tickets adult $59-69, child $39-49; 🕑 7:30pm & 10pm Sun-Fri; Ⓜ Harrah's/Imperial Palace; ♿

Vegas' top pop-star impersonator show features real talent – there is no lip-synching allowed. Video screens beside the stage show real-life concert clips of the performers, while the back-up dancers boogie up a *Saturday Night Fever* storm.

⭐ LOVE

☎ 792-7777, 800-963-9634; www.cirquedusoleil.com; Mirage, 3400 Las Vegas Blvd S; tickets $94-150; 🕑 7pm & 9:30pm Thu-Mon; Ⓜ Harrah's/Imperial Palace; ♿

Another smash hit from Cirque du Soleil, *LOVE* started off as the brainchild of the late George Harrison. Using Abbey Road master tapes, the show psychedelically fuses the musical legacy of the Beatles with Cirque's high-energy dancers and, of course, the troupe's signature aerial acrobats. With 360-degree seating, everyone gets a good view.

⭐ MYSTÈRE

☎ 894-7722, 800-392-1999; www.cirquedusoleil.com; TI (Treasure Island), 3300 Las Vegas Blvd S; tickets adult $60-109, child $30-55; 🕑 7pm & 9:30pm Sat-Wed; 🚌 Deuce; ♿

What Dalí did for painting, Cirque du Soleil aims to do for the stage. An oddball celebration of life begins with a pair of babies making their way in a world filled with weird creatures. A misguided clown's humorous antics are interspersed with agile feats of acrobats, aerialists and dancers. It's the cheapest Cirque ticket in town.

PHANTOM

☎ 414-9000, 866-641-7469; www. phantomlasvegas.com; Venetian, 3355 Las Vegas Blvd S; tickets $69-165; ☾ 7pm Mon-Sat, 9:30pm Mon & Sat; Ⓜ Harrah's/Imperial Palace; ♿

A drop-dead gorgeous theater mimics the opulent 19th-century Parisian opera house where this haunting musical about a doomed love triangle takes place. Boastfully renamed 'The Las Vegas Spectacular,' the Strip's version stars all-new special effects, from an onstage lake to exploding fireworks above. The VIP experience buys a backstage tour.

THE RAT PACK IS BACK!

☎ 386-2444; www.ratpackisback. com; Plaza, 1 Main St; tickets $57-88; ☾ 7:30pm nightly; 🚌 Deuce

Capitalizing on Rat Pack nostalgia, the show faithfully replicates the gang's routines, right down to the same songs, politically incorrect jokes and embarrassing behavior by Marilyn Monroe. Ol' Blue Eyes looks convincing, but you'll fall in love with Dino and the fantastic live band. If only the crowd had more young hipsters and fewer cranky senior citizens, it'd be aces.

VIVA ELVIS

☎ 877-253-5847; www.cirquedusoleil. com; Aria, 3730 Las Vegas Blvd S; tickets $99-175; ☾ 7pm & 9:30pm Fri-Wed; 🚌 Deuce

Cirque du Soleil's carnival of fun never stops on the Strip. Like the Beatles-themed *LOVE* (opposite), *Viva Elvis* is a musical journey through the life of The King of rock 'n' roll, full of chart-topping hits and 1950s-inspired choreography. Don't expect the high-flying acrobatics and aerial stunts of other Cirque shows, however. Stop by the official store (p98) for one-of-a-kind souvenirs.

SPAS & SALONS

Some day spas are reserved exclusively for hotel guests, especially on weekends. Day-use fees ($20 to $45) are normally waived for those receiving treatments ($100 to $200 per hour). Many spas have fitness facilities (bring workout clothes and shoes) and full-service beauty salons.

V

LAS VEGAS

PLAY

⭐ BATHHOUSE

☎ 877-632-9636; www.mandalaybay.com; THEhotel at Mandalay Bay, 3950 Las Vegas Blvd S; 🕙 6am-8pm; 🚌 Deuce

Seducing both sexes, this $25-million minimalist Asian-inspired spa offers redwood saunas, eucalyptus steam rooms and Ayurvedic herbal baths. Organic skincare products include an 'aromapothecary' of massage oils blended to match your personality.

⭐ CANYON RANCH SPACLUB

☎ 414-3600, 877-220-2688; www.canyonranch.com; 4th fl, Grand Canal Shoppes, Venetian, 3377 Las Vegas Blvd S; 🕙 6am-8pm, cafe 7am-2pm; 🚌 Harrah's/Imperial Palace

Popular for side-by-side couples' treatments, this health-minded place offers over 100 activities –

from deep-tissue massage to cocoon body wraps to indoor rock climbing – all priced à la carte. Rates drop midweek. Day passes cover 'Aquavana' hydro-spa baths, a steamy herbal laconium, co-ed salt grotto and more.

⭐ DRIFT SPA & HAMMAM

☎ 944-3219; www.palmsplace.com; Palms Place, 4381 W Flamingo Rd; 🕙 6am-9pm; 🚌 202

Make that nasty hangover disappear and let your mind unwind at this glam spa. Bathe yourself in steam at the co-ed traditional Turkish hammam (sorry, *not* clothing-optional), dip into the hot-soaking and cold-plunge pools, and get lost in the garden, where couples' treatment rooms are lit by aromatherapy candles after dark. Thermal detox and

The ultimate in pampering is offered at bathhouse. Go on...

Ayurvedic health remedies are available on demand.

⭐ KIM VÕ SALON

☎ 791-7474; www.kimvo.com; Mirage, 3400 Las Vegas Blvd S; ☀ 9am-7pm; Ⓜ Harrah's/Imperial Palace

Feel absolutely fabulous at celebrity stylist Kim Võ's salon while you get a champagne hair rinse under a disco ball or a makeover from the magic man himself, who has worked on pro athletes and US presidents.

⭐ QUA BATHS & SPA

☎ 731-7776, 866-782-0655; www .harrahs.com/qua; 2nd fl, Augustus Tower, Caesars Palace, 3570 Las Vegas Blvd S; ☀ 6am-8pm; Ⓜ Flamingo/ Caesars Palace

Social spa-going is encouraged at Qua (p22), which evokes the ancient Roman rituals of indulgent bathing. The spa's gossipy public areas include a tea lounge, herbal steam room, cedar sauna and arctic ice room, where artificial snowflakes fall. On the men's side, there's a barber spa and big-screen live-sports TVs.

⭐ RED ROCK SPA

☎ 797-7878, 866-363-2872; www .redrocklasvegas.com; Red Rock Casino Resort Spa, 11011 W Charleston Blvd at I-215; ☀ 6am-7pm; 🚌 206

Far-flung west of the Strip, this chic spa emphasizes holistic heal-ing practices and is best known for its adventure-spa menu, which features guided rock climbing in nearby Red Rock Canyon (p160). Order a specialty Thai massage or get rubbed down 'on the rocks' with heated river stones.

⭐ SPORTS

Although Vegas doesn't have any professional sports franchises, it's a city of die-hard sports fans. You can wager on just about anything at casinos' race and sports books (p39). Nearly every watering hole runs *Monday Night Football* specials, including downtown's Triple 7 brewpub (p137).

World-class championship boxing draws in fans from all over the globe; take a look at www.boxinginlasvegas.com for the latest news, ringside pics and fight schedules.

Auto racing at the Las Vegas Motor Speedway is enormously popular, especially during Nascar Weekend in March. The premier rodeo event of the year is the Wrangler National Finals Rodeo (p133), held every December. **UNLV Runnin' Rebels** (☎ 739-3267, 866-388-3267; www.unlvtickets.com) college football and basketball teams enjoy a patriotic local following. With a googly-eyed alien mascot, the minor-league **Las Vegas 51s**

(☎ 386-7200; www.lv51.com; Cashman Field, 850 Las Vegas Blvd N) baseball team, a franchise of the MLB Toronto Blue Jays, plays home games from late April through August. Affiliated with the NHL Phoenix Coyotes, the minor-league **Las Vegas Wranglers** (☎ 471-7825; www.lasvegaswranglers. com) ice-hockey team faces off at the Orleans Arena from October to April. If you adore watching bitchy, buxom girls on wheels, there's the riotous **Sin City Rollergirls** (www.sincity rollergirls.com; Las Vegas Roller Hockey Center, 800 Karen Ave) roller derby team.

STRIP CLUBS

Vegas is the original adult Disney-land. Prostitution may be illegal, but there are plenty of places offering the illusion of sex on demand. Unescorted women are not welcome at most clubs, especially not on busy nights. Bring cash for tips.

CRAZY HORSE 3

☎ 673-1700; www.crazyhorse3.com; 3525 W Russell Rd; cover $30; 🕐 24hr; 🚌 104

Not even the FBI's 'Operation G-Sting' (aka 'Strippergate') could

FORE!

There are dozens of spectacular golf courses in the Vegas Valley, most within 10 miles of the Strip. Golf season is in full swing from fall through spring (summers are just too darn hot!). For green-fee discounts and last-minute tee-time availability, contact **Las Vegas Preferred Tee Times** (☎ 877-255-7277; www.lvptt.com).

Angel Park (☎ 254-4653, 888-446-5358; www.angelpark.com; 100 S Rampart Blvd) Arnold Palmer–designed championship 18-hole courses, plus the 12-hole, par-3 Cloud Nine course (which is partially lit for night play).

Badlands (☎ 363-0754; www.badlandsgc.com; 9119 Alta Dr) Three nine-hole Troon Golf courses present the ultimate bad-ass desert challenge, with ball-chewing turf and unforgiving layouts.

Las Vegas Paiute Golf Resort (☎ 658-1400, 800-711-2833; www.lvpaiutegolf.com; 10325 Nu-Way Kaiv Blvd, off US95) A trio of scenic Pete Dye–designed courses in the Spring Mountains outside town.

Royal Links (☎ 450-8123, 888-427-6678; www.royallinksgolfclub.com; 5995 E Vegas Valley) A castle-like clubhouse (with a pub!) leads onto an 18-hole course inspired by famous British Open greens. Tiger Woods scored a record-setting 67 here.

Tournament Players Clubs Las Vegas (TPC; ☎ 256-2500; www.tpc.com/lasvegas; 9851 Canyon Run Dr) A PGA Tour stop, the Canyons course incorporates native desert vegetation, which requires minimal irrigation. It's also a certified Audubon cooperative sanctuary.

SPORTS & CONCERT MEGA VENUES

Las Vegas Motor Speedway (☎ 644-4444, 800-644-4444; www.lvms.com; 7000 Las Vegas Blvd N) Nascar, Indy racing, drag racing and race car ride-alongs (p83).

Mandalay Bay Events Center (☎ 632-7580; www.mandalaybay.com; 3950 Las Vegas Blvd S; 🚌 Deuce) Boxing, ultimate fighting and headliner concerts.

MGM Grand Garden Arena (☎ 891-7777, 877-880-0880; www.mgmgrand.com; 3799 Las Vegas Blvd S; Ⓜ MGM Grand) Boxing, superstar concerts and magic.

Orleans Arena (☎ 284-7777, 888-234-2334; www.orleansarena.com; Orleans, 4500 W Tropicana Ave; 🚌 201) Boxing, hockey, motorsports and concerts.

Sam Boyd Stadium (☎ 739-3267, 866-388-3267; www.unlvtickets.com; 7000 E Russell Rd) UNLV college football, motorsports and concerts.

South Point Events Center (☎ 797-8055; www.southpointeventscenter.com; 9777 Las Vegas Blvd S; 🚌 117) Equestrian events, boxing, motorcycle races and monster-truck jams.

Thomas & Mack Center (☎ 739-3267, 866-388-3267; www.unlvtickets.com; UNLV campus, Swenson St & E Tropicana Ave; 🚌 108) College basketball, boxing, concerts and rodeos.

Watch 'em burn rubber at Las Vegas Motor Speedway

GIRLS JUST WANNA HAVE FUN

The dancers at Rio's **Chippendales Theater** (☎ 777-7776; www.riolas vegas.com; admission $40-50) seem more concerned with basking in the spotlight than giving the girls a good time. Private sky boxes, Flirt cocktail lounge and a plush bathroom with a 'gossip pit' are the icing on the hunky cake. You can touch the lovely lads of Excalibur's **Thunder Down Under** (☎ 597-7600; www.excalibur.com; admission $40-50), who provide nonstop fun and flirting. At Planet Hollywood's Miracle Mile Shops (p94), VH1's award-winning **American Storm** (☎ 866-932-1818; www.vtheaterboxoffice.com; tickets $50-60) takes it off on weekends.

keep the doors of this legendary gentlemen's club, where porn star Jenna Jameson got started, closed forever. Moved to just off I-15, this adult playground has a hookah lounge, all-night sushi bar and live rock bands.

⭐ OLYMPIC GARDEN

☎ 385-9361; www.ogvegas.com; 1531 Las Vegas Blvd S; cover $30; ☼ 24hr; 🚌 Deuce

The unpretentious OG wins high marks from topless-club aficionados – and the nickname 'Silicone Valley' from the competition. Up to 50 dancers work the rooms at any given time, so there's something to please everyone. Studs strip upstairs for the ladies Wednesday through Sunday nights.

⭐ RICK'S CABARET

☎ 367-4000; www.lvscores.com; 3355 S Procyon St; cover $30; ☼ 24hr

Formerly Scores, the notorious NYC strip-club chain that Howard Stern raves about, Rick's Cabaret has taken over a building that looks like a miniature replica of Caesars Palace. Celebrity actors and pro athletes often drop by, though you probably won't catch a glimpse of 'em – they get their own private entrance. The premium cigar menu is superb.

⭐ SAPPHIRE

☎ 796-6000; www.sapphirelasvegas .com; 3025 S Industrial Rd; cover $30-50; ☼ 24hr; 🚌 213

Everything is larger than life at the 'world's largest adult entertainment complex,' with a stable of thousands of entertainers and VIP skyboxes overlooking the showroom that's cheesily dominated by a story-high martini glass. Beefy men strip upstairs in the Playgirl Club on Friday and Saturday nights.

ULTRA LOUNGES & AFTER HOURS

After-hours party spots and DJ events come and go, including at nightclubs like Krāve (p142).

⭐ BLUSH
☎ 770-3633; www.wynnlasvegas.com; Wynn, 3131 Las Vegas Blvd S; cover $20-30; 🕙 9pm-4am Tue-Sat; 🚍 Ace Gold
A long, narrow room beckons with glowing paper lanterns, gauzy drapery, candlelit tables, a starlight patio and premium VIP bottle service beside a boutique-sized onyx dance floor. The cover charge may be waived before midnight. Two more no-cover lounges nearby for smoochy drinks are Wynn's Parasol Up and lakeside Parasol Down.

⭐ CATHOUSE
☎ 262-4228; www.cathouselv.com; Luxor, 3900 Las Vegas Blvd S; 🕙 1am-6pm Wed, 10:30pm-4am Thu-Sat; 🚍 Deuce
Lingerie-clad coquettes tease, taunt and flaunt their bountiful assets at this low-lit ultra lounge, styled like a French bordello, where DJs spin. Stylish dress code.

⭐ DRAI'S
☎ 737-0555; www.drais.net; Bill's Gamblin' Hall & Saloon, 3595 Las Vegas Blvd S; cover $20-50; 🕙 1am-dawn Thu-Sun; 🚍 Flamingo/Caesars Palace
Ready for a scene straight outta Hollywood? Things don't really get going until after 4am here, when DJs spinning progressive discs keep the fashion plates who drape themselves on overstuffed sofas

from being too discontented. Strict dress code.

⭐ GHOSTBAR
☎ 942-6832; http://ghostbar-las-vegas.n9negroup.com; 55th fl, Palms Tower, Palms, 4321 W Flamingo Rd; cover $20-40; 🕙 8pm-3am; 🚍 202
With its 360-degree panoramas and sci-fi decor, the Palms' 55th-floor watering hole pulls in a clubby crowd thick with hip-hop stars and pro athletes. The lineup of hoochie mamas and wannabe gangstas can be tiresome, but the views are to die for. Dress to kill.

⭐ GOLD LOUNGE
☎ 693-8300; www.lightgroup.com; Aria, 3730 Las Vegas Blvd S; cover $20-50; 🕙 5pm-4am; 🚍 Deuce
Inspired by Elvis Presley's Memphis mansion, this deluxe black-and-gold nightspot has horsehair chairs, a stallion lamp that just begs to be ridden (just kidding!) and steerhorns hanging over the bar. DJs keep takin' care of business, as the King would say, all night. Fashionable attire required.

⭐ REVOLUTION LOUNGE
☎ 693-8300; www.thebeatlesrevolutionlounge.com; Mirage, 3400 Las Vegas Blvd S; cover $5-$20; 🕙 10pm-4am Wed-Mon; Ⓜ Harrah's/Imperial Palace
Fans of the original Fab Four can drop into this psychedelic

ALL WET

Las Vegas' outrageous pool-party season heats up the summer. Think of it as Ibiza in the desert: outdoor clubs with bikini-clad models, bumpin' DJs and bottle service. Expect hefty cover charges and long lines; queue early, especially on weekends. Our fave places to chill out poolside:

Bare (Mirage; p52) Adults-only pool lounge with mod chaise lounges, palm trees waving overhead, and cold fruit smoothies and hot tapas bites.

Ditch Fridays (Palms; p55) Skipping school or work has never seemed so seductive. An MTV-style, anything-goes atmosphere rules.

Rehab (Hard Rock; p48) A-list celebs, rock stars and costumed partiers are among the hordes lounging poolside on summer Sundays.

Tao Beach (Tao; p144) Tan yourself lying on daybeds or cool off inside high-tech cabanas that are outfitted with iPods and Xboxes.

Wet Republic Ultra Pool (MGM Grand; p51) Bathing beauties, rockin' DJs and pitchers of mojitos, plus valet parking practically poolside.

Beatles-themed ultra lounge created by Cirque du Soleil. DJs spin just about everything, from down-tempo house, Brit pop, hip-hop and world-music fusion to mash-ups of classic rock and '80s new wave. The no-cover Abbey Road Bar out front opens at noon daily.

Explore the breathtaking Red Rock Canyon (p160), only a 40-minute drive from the Strip

GRAND CANYON NATIONAL PARK

The Grand Canyon is the USA's best-known natural attraction. Measuring over 275 miles long and more than a mile deep, it's an incredible spectacle of Technicolor rock strata. After initially being dismissed by Spanish conquistadors and Western pioneers as little more than an obstacle to exploration, in the late 19th century the canyon drew miners bent on exploiting its natural resources. Later tourists arrived seeking a romanticized wilderness ideal as they embraced the canyon's beauty. When President Theodore Roosevelt visited in 1903, he sagely remarked, 'You cannot improve on it.'

Carved by the Colorado River, the canyon's peaks, buttes and rims give access to fantastic vistas. Descending into its depths on hiking and mule-riding trails reveals an amazing variety of landscape, wildlife and climates. If your time is limited, flightseeing day trips from Las Vegas (often combined with flyovers of Hoover Dam and Lake Mead, and a bus tour of the South Rim) can introduce you to this gob-stopping hole in the ground.

Although the canyon's rims are only 10 miles apart as the condor flies, it's a 215-mile, five-hour drive on narrow roads between the South and North

The stunning vista of the Grand Canyon from the South Rim at Hopi Point

Rim visitor centers. The **South Rim** is the most popular jumping-off point for exploring the national park, where there is no escaping the crowds between May and September. Though the South Rim receives over 90% of the four million park visitors each year, the **North Rim** is not far from Zion and Bryce Canyon National Parks, making it a more memorable road trip, scenery-wise.

Approaching the South Rim, **Mather Point** near Canyon View Information Plaza gives you an exhilarating first look at the canyon's grandeur. After stretching your legs, drive north to **Grand Canyon Village**. Peruse Native American crafts inside **Hopi House**, designed by innovative Western architect Mary Colter; have cocktails on the back porch of the majestic **El Tovar Hotel**; and peruse the art displays inside **Kolb Studio**. For panoramic views of the canyon's geological layer cake, head over to **Yavapai Observation Station.** Of course, the foremost attraction is the canyon rim itself, paralleled on the south side by a 33-mile paved scenic drive. The canyon dips in and out of view as the road passes through the piñon-juniper and ponderosa pine forests. Pullouts along the way offer jaw-dropping views, and interpretive signs explain about natural history. Between March and November, only shuttle buses may travel along Hermit Rd west of the village. To the east, Desert View Dr is open to cars year-round. The latter takes you past the 800-year-old pueblo ruins behind the **Tusayan Museum** of Native American history and culture, and the enchanting five-story-high **Desert View Watchtower**, which is the highest point on the South Rim. On the North Rim, rugged 4WD roads lead to more remote viewpoints.

To get away from the traffic, you can day-hike partway down to the Colorado River, or stay overnight at Phantom Ranch, where reservations are a must. Mule rides and river-rafting trips also require advance planning.

INFORMATION

Location 275 miles east of Las Vegas
Getting there 🚗 From the Strip: for South Rim (five hours), take I-15 south to I-215 east to US 93 south to I-40 east to AZ 64 north to Grand Canyon Village; for North Rim (5½ hours), take I-15 north to UT 9 east to UT 59 south to AZ 389 south to US 89 Alt (89-A) south to AZ 67 south
Contact ☎ 928-638-7888; www.nps.gov/grca
Cost per vehicle for a seven-day pass $25
When to go South Rim ⏾ 24/7/365; North Rim ⏾ mid-May–mid-Oct
Eating South Rim: Arizona Room (☎ 928-638-2631; Bright Angel Lodge); North Rim: Grand Canyon Lodge Dining Room (☎ 928-638-2611)

HOOVER DAM, LAKE MEAD & VALLEY OF FIRE

Once the tallest in the world, the art-deco Hoover Dam is an engineering marvel, its graceful concrete curve filling a dramatic canyon backed by brilliant blue waters. The dam was built primarily to control floods on the lower Colorado River, which irrigates a million acres of land in the USA and half a million in Mexico.

Bus tours from Las Vegas are a good deal and guarantee a ticket for the tour, which lets you ride an elevator more than 50 stories down to see the massive power generators, then zoom back up to view the exhibit halls, outdoor spillways and Winged Figures of the Republic memorial.

When you tire of admiring the view and pretending to jump the railing (no terrorist jokes, please – that sort of thing is taken *very* seriously around here), backtrack a few miles to **Lake Mead National Recreation Area** (☎ 702-293-8990; www.nps.gov/lame; admission per car $5; ☽ 24hr), where a scenic shoreline drive passes hiking trails, beaches, marinas and birding spots, all the way up to Overton's **Lost City Museum** (☎ 702-397-2193; http://museums. nevadaculture.org; 721 S Moapa Valley Blvd; adult/child $5/free; ☽ 8:30am-4:30pm Thu-Sun) of Native American culture. The museum is north of the turn off to **Valley of Fire State Park** (☎ 702-397-2088; http://parks.nv.gov/vf.htm; admission per car $10; ☽ 24hr), a masterpiece of Southwest desert scenery with psychedelic sandstone carved by wind and water (**Atlatl Rock** has Native American petroglyphs, too). Detour to **White Domes**, passing **Rainbow Vista** and the side road to **Fire Canyon** and **Silica Dome** (where Star Trek's Captain Kirk perished).

INFORMATION

Location 30 miles southeast of Las Vegas
Getting there 🚌 From the Strip (45 minutes): I-15 south to I-215 east to I-515/US 93 & 95; follow US 93 east of Boulder City
Contact ☎ 702-494-2517; www.usbr.gov/lc/hooverdam
Cost Hoover Dam tours from $11/9, parking garage $7
When to go Hoover Dam visitor center ☽ 9am-5pm (to 6pm in summer), last tickets sold 45min before closing; Lake Mead & Valley of Fire visitor centers ☽ 8:30am-4:30pm

Vertigo-inducing Hoover Dam

OUT OF TOWN

RED ROCK CANYON

The 130-sq-mile Red Rock Canyon National Conservation Area (pictured right) should be on everyone's must-see list, but fortunately isn't. The startling contrast between the Strip's artificial neon glow and the awesome natural forces of the canyon can't be exaggerated.

Created about 65 million years ago, the canyon is more like a valley, with a steep, rugged escarpment rising 3000ft on its western edge. A 13-mile, one-way **scenic driving and cycling loop** passes by its most striking natural features and panoramic viewpoints. Rugged hiking trails lead to seasonal waterfalls. The **Calico Hills** area is the premier place for rock climbing. The popular **Willow Springs** picnic area offers nature walks. To ride 'em cowboy, make reservations with **Cowboy Trail Rides** (☎ 702-387-2457; www.cowboytrailrides.com).

Before reaching Red Rock Canyon, you'll drive by the dusty town of Blue Diamond, where **McGhie's Bike Outpost** (☎ 702-875-4820; http://mcghies.com; 16 Cottonwood #B; ✪ call for hours) is a one-stop shop for rentals (per day $40 to $65), guided tours around Red Rock Canyon, and directions for more than 125 miles of single track in the Cottonwood Valley and Black Velvet areas. North along NV 159, **Spring Mountain Ranch State Park** (☎ 702-875-4141; http://parks.nv.gov/smr.htm; per car $9; ✪ 8am-dusk, visitor center 10am-4pm), once owned by eccentric billionaire Howard Hughes, offers nature walks, ranch tours and historical exhibits. Nearby **Bonnie Springs** (☎ 702-875-4191; www.bonniesprings.com; 1 Gunfighter Lane; per car $20; ✪ 10:30am-6pm Wed-Sun, shorter hours in winter), the scene of countless B-movie shoots, is a touristy sideshow for the kiddies.

INFORMATION
Location 25 miles west of Las Vegas
Getting there 🚗 From the Strip (40 minutes): I-15 south to Blue Diamond Rd (NV 160), then west to NV 159
Contact ☎ 702-515-5350; www.blm.gov
Cost per car/bicycle $7/3
When to go Visitor center ✪ 8am-4:30pm, scenic loop ✪ 7am-7pm Mar, 6am-8pm Apr-Sep, 6am-7pm Oct, 6am-5pm Nov-Feb
Eating Hash House A Go Go (p126), LBS Burger Joint (p126)

TAKE A TOUR

Free Strip hotel pick-ups and drop-offs are included with most tours; check online for deep discounts. Hour-long air tours of the Grand Canyon cost from $125 per person; day-long air/ground combos (including the Skywalk) start from $230, while premier helicopter tours landing on the canyon's floor fetch over $315. For city tours, see p193.

Adventure Las Vegas (☎ 888-867-6259; www.adventurelasvegas.com; tours $119-355; reservations 24hr) One-stop shop for adventure tours; arranges everything from sunset horseback rides and Lake Mead kayaking trips to desert mountain-biking and zipline tours.

Black Canyon River Adventures (☎ 294-1414, 800-455-3490; www.blackcanyon adventures.com; Hacienda Hotel & Casino, US 93, Boulder City; tours from $86/54) Take a three-hour motor-assisted raft journey down the Colorado River, launching from the base of Hoover Dam.

Boulder City Outfitters (☎ 293-1190, 800-748-3702; http://bouldercityoutfitters.com; 111 Veterans Memorial Dr, Boulder City; guided hike/kayak tours $100/150, canoe or kayak rental per day $35-75, paddlers' shuttle $10-50) Guided kayak tours (two-person minimum) launch from the base of Hoover Dam, with stops at hot springs and waterfalls; shuttle service available for DIY paddlers.

Escape Adventures (☎ 596-2953, 800-596-2953; www.escapeadventures.com; day/weekend trips from $100/499) Escape the city's neon jungle for a mountain-biking, road-cycling, hiking or multisport adventure tour of Red Rock Canyon or national parks.

Gray Line (☎ 384-1234, 800-634-6579; www.graylinelasvegas.com; tours $55-159) Reputable tour-bus operator offers a variety of excursions to Hoover Dam and the Grand Canyon, as well as Colorado River floats and Lake Mead cruises.

Papillon Grand Canyon Helicopters (☎ 736-7243, 888-635-7272; www.papillon.com; McCarran Executive Terminal, 275 E Tropicana Ave; bus/flightseeing tours from $79/175) Vegas' original helicopter-flightseeing outfitter does luxury tours of the Grand Canyon; its motorcoach tours of the South Rim stop en route at Hoover Dam.

Pink Jeep Tours (☎ 895-6777, 888-900-4480; www.pinkjeeplasvegas.com; 3629 W Hacienda Ave; half-day tours $89-129, full-day tours $135-359) Arranges small-group trips to Hoover Dam, Red Rock Canyon, Valley of Fire, Mt Charleston, Death Valley, Zion National Park and the Grand Canyon's North Rim or Skywalk.

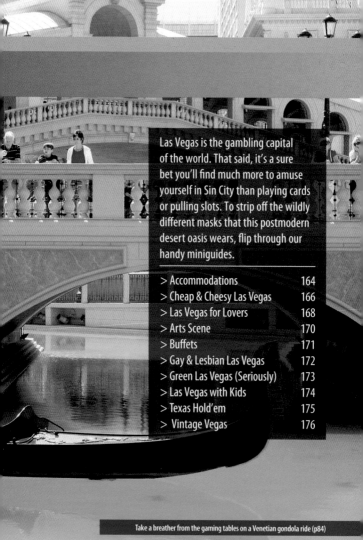

Las Vegas is the gambling capital of the world. That said, it's a sure bet you'll find much more to amuse yourself in Sin City than playing cards or pulling slots. To strip off the wildly different masks that this postmodern desert oasis wears, flip through our handy miniguides.

Take a breather from the gaming tables on a Venetian gondola ride (p84)

ACCOMMODATIONS

Vegas hits the jackpot, with almost 150,000 guest rooms. Even if a bankroll isn't burning a hole in your pocket, a little luxury can be had more cheaply here than almost anywhere else in the world. Of course an exquisite penthouse villa overlooking Las Vegas Blvd (aka the Strip), with perks such as 24-hour butler service, costs thousands of dollars per night.

On your first trip to Las Vegas, almost any casino hotel on the Strip will bedazzle, but don't go by name recognition alone. The Center Strip is where most of the magnificent megaresorts and the hottest action is, and you'll pay for it. The South Strip is a comfy compromise: you'll get the full Vegas experience, but for less dough. Some famous casino hotels on the North Strip have the most disappointing rooms and location. Downtown is for local gamblers and penny-pinchers who've tired of the Strip scene. Outlying-area hotels offer some deals, if you're willing to make the trip.

Whatever you do, don't arrive without a reservation. It's amazing how often every hotel in town is booked solid. Year-round, room rates average

Need a place to stay? Find and book it at lonelyplanet.com. Around 50 properties are featured for Las Vegas – each personally visited, thoroughly reviewed and happily recommended by a Lonely Planet author. From hostels to high-end hotels, we've hunted out the places that will bring you unique and special experiences. Read independent reviews by authors and other travelers, and get practical information including amenities, maps and photos. Then reserve your room simply and securely via Hotels & Hostels – our online booking service. It's all at lonelyplanet.com/hotels.

50% less from Sunday through Thursday nights. Unless you're on a junket, avoid visiting during the biggest conventions, when hotel rates shoot sky-high. The slowest times of year are during the excruciatingly hot summer (June, July and August) and the coldest winter months. If you're claustrophobic, pass on New Year's Eve and other major holidays (p192).

If you're looking for a lower rate or want to stay at a hotel that's sold out, check back in a few days or a week or two. Sometimes you can suddenly reserve rooms for much less than you'd been quoted before. It also pays to check with the hotel you've booked a few days before your trip starts to see if the rates you were quoted have changed, and if they've fallen, ask that your reservation rate be lowered, too.

WEB RESOURCES

Discounted room rates are found on the casino hotels' own websites, Facebook and Twitter pages, or at online travel discounters like www.travelworm.com. The **Las Vegas Convention & Visitors Authority** (☎ 877-847-4858; www.visitlasvegas.com) can help with last-minute accommodations.

LAS VEGAS' HIPPEST HOTELS

> Aria (www.arialasvegas.com)
> Hard Rock (www.hardrockhotel.com)
> THEhotel at Mandalay Bay (www.thehotelatmandalaybay.com)
> Palms Place (www.palmsplace.com)
> Red Rock (www.redrocklasvegas.com)

LAS VEGAS' MOST LUXURIOUS SUITES

> Mandarin Oriental (www.mandarin oriental.com/lasvegas)
> Palazzo (www.palazzolasvegas.com)
> Palms & Palms Place (www.palms.com)
> Skylofts at MGM Grand (www.skyloftsmgmgrand.com)
> Trump International Hotel (www.trumplasvegas.com)

LAS VEGAS' COOLEST HOTEL POOLS

> Bellagio (www.bellagio.com)
> Caesars Palace (www.caesarspalace.com)
> Flamingo (www.flamingolasvegas.com)
> Mandalay Bay (www.mandalaybay.com)
> MGM Grand (www.mgmgrand.com)

LAS VEGAS' BEST BARGAIN HOTELS

> Golden Nugget (www.goldennugget.com)
> Main Street Station (www.mainstreetcasino.com)
> Orleans (www.orleanscasino.com)
> South Point (www.southpointcasino.com)
> Tropicana (www.troplv.com)

Top left Life's pretty sweet at the Mandarin Oriental's Dynasty Suite

SNAPSHOTS

CHEAP & CHEESY LAS VEGAS

Elvis and Liberace have long gone to their graves, and Siegfried and Roy are no longer performing on the Strip with their white tigers, but Las Vegas still has plenty of wacky and way-out, tacky and trashy stuff to see and do. Best of all, much of it won't cost you a thing.

Some critics lament that everything in Las Vegas is in outrageously bad taste, and, of course, that's often true. But that's something to celebrate, too. It's as much fun to dive into the city's unbelievably campy depths as it is to aim for its high-rollin' luxury heights.

So, when you're down to your last dime, don't despair. Spend all day watching the gob-stopping free casino spectaculars (p80) and inhaling the (almost free) food and drinks. Did you know they'll serve you free booze even if you're just playing the 'Penny Alley' slot machines? It's true.

Speed down the Strip, which is a free-for-all freak show, day and night. Gawk at the Mirage's exploding faux-Polynesian volcano (p81). Get your free kicks watching the sexy hijinks of the *Sirens of TI* mock pirate battle (p81). Check out Marilyn Monroe and Elvis impersonators performing at the Imperial Palace (p78).

Hold-outs from the 1950s and '60s, a few kitschy casino hotels survive at the far north end of the Strip. Circus Circus (p44) definitely wins the prize for the cheesiest casino theme. Pick up a 'fun book' full of discount coupons at the hilariously tacky Slots A' Fun (p80) next door. Across the street, grab a tropical drink at the garishly neon-lit Fireside Lounge (p134), which is attached to the Peppermill casino's 24-hour coffee shop. If you're still rarin' to go for a low-roller's ride, there's no better place to keep the party going strong than on downtown's Fremont Street Experience (p80).

Last but not least, pay your respects to the maestro of flamboyant kitsch, Liberace, at his off-Strip memorial museum (p79), where fanatical 'Red Hatters' keep the candles of his outrageous shrine burning bright.

VEGAS' KITSCHIEST SOUVENIRS

> At-home gaming paraphernalia from the Gamblers General Store (p99)
> Casino-themed cocktail glasses (eg plastic Eiffel Tower from Paris Las Vegas, colorful ceramic showgirl stein from Bally's)
> Full-sized Elvis cardboard cut-out from Bonanza Gifts (p98)

> G-string, go-go boots or an erotic toy from a naughty novelty shop (p90)
> Showgirl's feather boa from Rainbow Feather Dyeing Co (p99)

CHEESIEST VEGAS ATTRACTIONS

> Circus Circus Midway (p80)
> Fremont Street Experience (p80)
> Haunted Vegas Tours (p193)
> Liberace Museum (p79)
> Viva Las Vegas Weddings (p85)

Top left Looking for that snow globe to complete the collection? Visit Bonanza Gifts (p98) **Above** Dice for every occasion at Gamblers General Store (p99)

SNAPSHOTS

LAS VEGAS FOR LOVERS

There must be something magical about Las Vegas for lovers, because a blushing couple ties the knot here every five minutes. Scores of celebrity couples have exchanged vows in Sin City, from Elvis Presley and Priscilla Beaulieu, to Sammy Davis Jr and Swedish model May Britt, to Andre Agassi and Steffi Graf. Why not you, too? After all, the 50-50 odds of a marriage surviving 'till death us do part' start to look pretty good in comparison to the chances of hitting a royal flush at the poker table. (You don't have to be sober to get married here either – that helps some folks a lot.)

Choices for the perfect spot to say 'I do' are endless. Weddings are performed in gondolas (p84) at the Venetian or atop the Eiffel Tower (p82) at Paris Las Vegas. You can hire an Elvis impersonator to serenade you with 'Blue Hawaii,' or dress up like Marilyn Monroe. You can even get married after a dramatic helicopter landing on the floor of the Grand Canyon (p85).

To be truthful, the more Vegas wedding chapels (p84) you see, the less you may be inclined to entrust them with the happiest day of your lives. Many are pretty tacky, full of plastic flowers, fake stained-glass windows and doll's-house pews. You'll feel rushed, as these places crank out dozens of weddings every day. Expect to pay at least $99 for a basic ceremony, including a chintzy limo ride to the chapel.

Before you get hitched at a wedding chapel, stop by Clark County's **Marriage Bureau** (☎ 671-0600; www.accessclarkcounty.com/depts/clerk/Pages/marriage_information.aspx; 201 E Clark Ave; ☙ 8am-midnight) for a license ($60 to $65).

Overseas visitors should check back home first to see if they'll need any additional documentation to 'make it official.'

Valentine's Day and New Year's Day are crush times for Vegas wedding chapels; if you want to say your vows at peak times, apply for a license up to a year in advance online. Make wedding-chapel reservations as far in advance as possible, too. Otherwise, civil courthouse ceremonies are performed 8am to 10pm daily.

You don't have to elope to find romance in Sin City. Steal a kiss over megamartinis atop the Stratosphere Tower (p132), clasp hands as you watch the Bellagio's dancing fountains show (p80) or hide out with your paramour in a luxe suite all weekend (p26). Room service menus feature champagne, gourmet chocolate and XXX goodies to spice up your love life.

If you're looking to explore your wilder side, Sin City infamously offers fantasy strip clubs (p150) and erotica shops (p90), all just a short cab ride away from the Strip. Or catch eye-popping burlesque acts, go-go dancers and topless showgirl revues at many casino hotels.

BEST SECRET SMOOCHING SPOTS
> Downtown Cocktail Room (p134)
> Fireside Lounge (p134)
> Mandarin Bar & Tea Lounge (City-Center; p136)
> Mix (p137)
> Vegas Wedding Chapel (p85)

MOST ROMANTIC FRENCH RESTAURANTS
> Alizé (p125)
> Joël Robuchon (p108)
> Mon Ami Gabi (p113)
> Restaurant Guy Savoy (p104)
> Twist by Pierre Gagnaire (p105)

Top left Get cozy at Fireside Lounge (p134) **Above** Be romanced in the plush, intimate surrounds of Joël Robuchon (p108)

ARTS SCENE

If art imitates life, then Las Vegas must be a masterpiece, because it strives to imitate everywhere else on earth. It has a miniature Eiffel Tower, mock-medieval castles, and Greek, Italian and Egyptian statuary copied from the masters. World-class exhibitions hit the Bellagio Gallery of Fine Art (p74). Downtown galleries (p74), especially in the 18b Arts District, are where you'll find works by local artists, especially on First Friday nights (p14).

Don't forget about Las Vegas' most famous art form: there are over 15,000 miles of neon tubing used for signage throughout the city. Start your DIY night-time neon art tour at the 'Welcome to Fabulous Las Vegas Nevada' sign (p81), then cruise the casinos of the Strip and downtown's Glitter Gulch, detouring to the Neon Museum (p76).

When it comes to live music (p139), casinos still book legendary entertainers just like in the 1950s and early '60s, when Frank Sinatra and his Rat Pack packed the house full. A few breakthrough local alt-rock bands have catapulted onto the national scene recently, such as the Killers and Panic! At the Disco. Catch up-and-coming sounds in the Fremont East entertainment district at the Beauty Bar (p134).

Hollywood fawns over Las Vegas, which is no surprise given that it's a half-day's drive from LA. Although currently on hiatus, CineVegas (p132) is a rising star on the indie film-festival circuit. For movies made here, see p186.

BEST ART GALLERIES
> Bellagio Gallery of Fine Art (p74)
> Brett Wesley Gallery (see p74)
> Commerce Street Studios (p76)
> Contemporary Arts Center (Arts Factory; p74)
> Neon Museum (p76)

COOLEST CASINO MIMETIC ARCHITECTURE
> Caesars Palace (p43)
> Luxor (p49)
> New York–New York (p53)
> Paris Las Vegas (p56)
> Venetian (p62; pictured above)

BUFFETS

Veterans of Vegas' 'groaning boards' proffer some sage words of advice. First, starve yourself for as long as possible before saddling up at a buffet, and don't count on eating any meals afterward. You'll get more for your money at breakfast or lunch – or better yet, weekend brunch – than at dinner, unless special entrées like steak or seafood are added.

Generally speaking, the more expensive the casino hotel, the better the fare. Famous buffets at Wynn (p117), Bellagio (p102), Planet Holly-wood (p114), Paris Las Vegas (p113), the M Resort (p125) and Palms Place (p55) compete for top honors. If you're a glutton for punishment, some casino hotels offer all-day buffet passes (from $30).

Once you wait out the queue at most buffets, the time-tested strategy is to grab teensy servings of everything before deciding what you really want to gorge on. Why get stuck with soggy sushi when a snappy chef is making fresh crepes or carving succulent roasted meats just a few food stations over? Always save room for multiple mini-desserts, from floating islands of caramel meringue to house-made gelato.

Oh, and don't forget to leave behind at least a dollar or two per person for the servers who bussed all those gluttonous piles of scrap-ridden plates off your table. It's only fair.

Fill your plate with global delicacies at Spice Market Buffet (p114)

GAY & LESBIAN LAS VEGAS

Nicknamed the Fruit Loop, the epicenter of Sin City's queer nightlife is about a mile east of the Strip, along Paradise Rd south of Harmon Ave and the Hard Rock casino hotel. Most bars, clubs and drag showrooms found here are oriented toward men, but host women-only nights. A more stealth gay scene orbits the Commercial Center, east of the Strip on Sahara Ave. Gay megaclub Krāve (p142) is the Strip's only predominantly queer venue.

Annual events include **Las Vegas Pride** (www.lasvegaspride.org) in May, and **gay rodeo events** (www.ngra.com), too. To plug into the city's current scene, **QVegas** (www.qvegas.com) offers online downloads of the monthly magazine, which is also freely available at **Get Booked** (☎ 737-7780; www.getbooked.com; 4640 S Paradise Rd; ☉ 10am-midnight Sun-Thu, 10am-2am Fri & Sat). Community websites include www.outinlasvegas.com and www.gayvegastravel.com. For social outings with local lesbians, join **Betty's Outrageous Adventures** (www.bettysout.com).

Although Vegas has a reputation as a wild party spot, most of its residents vote conservative. Same-sex public displays of affection aren't common or much appreciated by the moral majority in this conservative town. Same-sex marriages aren't recognized by the state of Nevada, although domestic partnerships are.

BEST BETS FOR LGBT NIGHTLIFE
> FreeZone (p135; pictured above)
> Krāve (p142)
> Piranha (p143)

BEST QUEER-FRIENDLY ATTRACTIONS & SHOWS
> Any Cirque du Soleil show (p144)
> Céline Dion (p144)
> Divas Las Vegas (p145)
> *Jubilee!* Backstage Tour (p146)
> Liberace Museum (p79)

GREEN LAS VEGAS (SERIOUSLY)

Las Vegas (in Spanish, 'the meadows') lies at the edge of the vast Mojave Desert. In the parched rain shadow of the Great Basin, this flat city inhabits a bowl-shaped valley surrounded by mountain ranges. The population of the city already numbers over half a million, and if you count outlying suburbs and independent cities, the total number of people in the metro area is fast approaching two million, more than double what it was just 15 years ago. Astoundingly, visitors outnumber locals nearly 20:1.

Because Las Vegas is an artificial playground built in the middle of the desert, is it any surprise that the valley may drain its entire water supply by the year 2021? Air pollution is another serious problem. The sky above the Strip is sometimes so dirty that you can't see the mountains for the haze. (For more on the city's environmental issues, see p184.)

But there's hope. An environmentally conscious educational complex, the Springs Preserve (p24 and p76) is literally a breath of fresh air. While other green spaces inside the city limits are rare, a few casino hotels have gardens (p77) for making your escape from the smoke-filled gaming areas. Along the Strip, ride the monorail (p190), a zero-emissions public transportation option. For excursions out of town, the Grand Canyon (p156), Red Rock Canyon (p160), Lake Mead and the Valley of Fire (p158) will satisfy your nature-loving soul.

The Springs Preserve is a major ecological achievement (p24 and p76)

SNAPSHOTS

LAS VEGAS WITH KIDS

Las Vegas half-heartedly sells itself as a family vacation destination. Because the legal gambling age is 21, many casino hotels and resorts would rather you simply left the little ones at home. Some high-end casino hotels even prohibit strollers from being on their grounds. State law prevents all minors from being in the gaming areas at all times.

Now, here's the good news. Las Vegas is full of family-friendly attractions and activities. Most casinos have virtual-reality and video game arcades, where even adults can have fun, such as at New York–New York, where a roller coaster shoots out of the Coney Island Emporium (p82), or Circus Circus' Adventuredome (p81). Teens will get a thrill atop the Stratosphere Tower (p84) and at Pole Position Raceway (p83). Some of the Strip's stage shows (including magic acts) welcome all-ages audiences. Speaking of which, kids can learn to do their own tricks at Houdini's Magic Shop (p98). For a fun, multimedia educational experience, make time to head out to the Springs Preserve (p24). Mandalay Bay's Shark Reef aquarium (p78; pictured below) and the MGM Grand's lion habitat (p77) are entertaining, as is the old-fashioned West Wind Las Vegas 5 Drive-In (p138). Out-of-town excursions, especially to the Grand Canyon (p156), make for unforgettable family adventures. Surf to www.kidsinvegas.com for more city-specific advice and information.

BEST KID-FRIENDLY STAGE SHOWS	FAST FAMILY-FRIENDLY EATS
> Kà (p145)	> BLT Burger (p109)
> LOVE (p146)	> Canter's Deli (p115)
> Mac King (p138)	> Luv-It Frozen Custard (p120)
> Mystère (p146)	> Metro Pizza (p123)
> Phantom (p147)	> Village Eateries (p110)

TEXAS HOLD'EM

A decade ago, Las Vegas visitors had a hard time finding a poker game. Many casinos, armed with profitability studies developed by MBAs, were replacing their card tables with high-limit slot machines. Ten years later, it's still hard to get a game in Vegas, but for an entirely different reason: poker has become the hottest game in town.

If you're one of those people who grew up playing wild draw poker games where the deuces, treys, one-eyed jacks, suicide kings and the queen who's not looking at the flower are all wild, you're in for a bit of a shock. While it's not the only game in town, Texas Hold'em is the most common. It's a fairly easy game to learn, but remarkably difficult to play well. Psychology helps.

The rules are simple. Each player is dealt two cards face down, known as hole cards. After a round of betting, three more cards – the 'flop' – are dealt face-up in the center of the table. These cards are community cards, shared by all the players still in the hand. After another round of betting, a fourth community card – the 'turn' – is dealt. After another round of betting, the fifth and final community card – the much-anticipated 'river' – is laid on the table. One last round of betting ensues, and the remaining players turn over their hole cards. The player who makes the strongest five-card hand (by combining his or her hole cards with three out of the five community cards) takes the pot.

TOP-RATED POKER ROOMS
> Binion's (p64)
> Golden Nugget (p47)
> MGM Grand (p51)
> Venetian (p62)
> Wynn (p63)

BEST POKER READS
> *All In: The (Almost) Entirely True Story of the World Series of Poker* (Jonathan Grotenstein & Storms Reback, 2005)
> *Cowboys Full: The Story of Poker* (James McManus, 2009)
> *Outplaying the Boys: Poker Tips for Competitive Women* (Cat Hulbert, 2005)
> *Poker: The Real Deal* (Phil Gordon & Jonathan Grotenstein, 2004)
> *Winning Low-Limit Hold'Em* (Lee Jones, 2005)

VINTAGE VEGAS

When it comes to Old Vegas, the slogan is 'Here today, gone tomorrow.' In a city that moves as fast as this one, priceless pieces of history get lost, bulldozed, imploded and discarded every day. So, if you want to devote a little time to unraveling the past in the present, hurry up and come see it while you still can.

Nothing says vintage Vegas more than the iconic 'Welcome to Fabulous Las Vegas Nevada' sign (see the boxed text, p81) south of the Strip. Except for maybe the Strip's original 1940s-era glam casino hotel, the Flamingo (p46), aka the folly that Bugsy built. Be sure to check out the yesteryear photos of movie stars and mobsters hidden by the valet-parking stand. At Bally's, you can catch a *Jubilee!* show (p145) after taking a behind-the-scenes tour led by a real showgirl or chorus boy (p146). East of the Strip at the Liberace Museum (p79), you can revel in more outlandish retro costumes.

If it's Elvis impersonators you're dying to see, search out the 'dealer-tainers' at the Imperial Palace (p78). Or you might catch sight of the King strolling along Las Vegas Blvd, past vintage casinos like the Sahara (p59) and wedding chapels (p84) galore, or near downtown's Fremont Street Experience (p80), the heart of historic Glitter Gulch (p19). There the Golden Gate casino hotel (p65) has been encouraging vice since 1906. Classier carpet joints like the Golden Nugget (p47) also have the sweet stench of Fabulous '50s glamour. You can play some good ol' no-limit poker with old-school cowboys in the back room at landmark Binion's (p64). Fremont St is a great place to search out spectacularly restored historical neon signs, too, courtesy of the Neon Museum (p76).

Get swept up in the nostalgia of the Sahara (p59)

>BACKGROUND

Find your *joie de vivre* at Paris Las Vegas (p56)

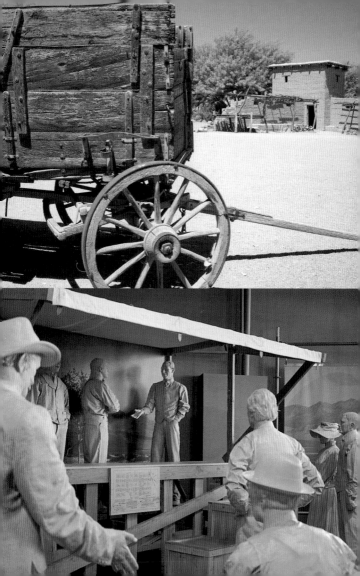

BACKGROUND
HISTORY

'What history?' you ask. Unlike the rest of the ruin-laden US Southwest, traces of Las Vegas' early history are scarce. Uto-Aztecan-speaking Southern Paiute tribespeople of Native Americans inhabited the Las Vegas Valley for over a millennium before the Spanish Trail was blazed through this last area of the country to be explored by Europeans.

Contrary to Hollywood legend, there was much more at this crossroads in the Mojave Desert than a few ramshackle gambling houses, tumbleweeds and cacti the day that mobster Benjamin 'Bugsy' Siegel opened the tropical-themed Flamingo casino hotel under the searing desert sun.

TAMING THE FRONTIER

In 1829 Rafael Rivera, a scout for a Mexican trading expedition, was likely the first outsider to locate the natural springs in the Las Vegas Valley. Another traveler along the Spanish Trail, US Army officer John C Fremont arrived in 1844 to explore and map the area. Amid the hard-scrabble legions of miners who arrived later in the mid-19th century was a group of men hell-bent on doing God's work in Indian country. These Mormons were sent from Salt Lake City by leader Brigham Young to colonize the state of Deseret, their spiritual homeland. Their fort stood here for only two years. After the Civil War, small farms and ranches flourished in the valley.

In 1905 the driving of a golden spike in Southern Nevada signaled the completion of a railroad linking Salt Lake City to Los Angeles (LA). Over two days, pioneers and real-estate speculators from LA bid for land, and lots in the Las Vegas townsite sold for up to 10 times their original price.

WEBSITES FOR PEEKING INTO THE PAST

> Classic Las Vegas (www.classiclasvegas.com)
> The First 100 (www.1st100.com)
> Las Vegas: An Unconventional History (www.pbs.org/wgbh/amex/lasvegas)
> Las Vegas Sun: History (www.lasvegassun.com/history)
> UNLV Special Collections (www.library.unlv.edu/speccol)

Top Left For a taste of the past, visit the Old Las Vegas Mormon Fort State Historic Park, north of downtown **Bottom Left** Take a history lesson at Springs Preserve (p24 and p76)

BEST TOWN BY A DAM SITE

As the dust settled, the city of Las Vegas was officially founded. Sin quickly took root in a downtown red-light district known as Block 16. Home to gambling, booze and prostitution, this row of saloons, with their makeshift 'cribs' (brothels) out back, survived Nevada's several bans on gambling and the supposedly 'dry' years of Prohibition.

The federally sponsored Boulder (later Hoover) Dam project and the legalization of gambling carried Las Vegas through the Great Depression that followed the stock-market crash of 1929. Lax divorce requirements, quickie weddings, legalized prostitution and championship boxing bouts proved money-making bets for local boosters. New Deal dollars kept flowing into Southern Nevada's coffers right through WWII, which brought a huge air-force base to town, plus a paved highway to LA.

THE FABULOUS FIFTIES

Along with the rest of America, post-WWII Las Vegas felt like a boomtown again. Backed by East Coast mob money, gangster Benjamin 'Bugsy' Siegel opened the $6-million Flamingo casino hotel in 1946. With its incandescent pastel paint job, tuxedoed janitors, Hollywood entertainers and flashing neon, it became the model for the new Las Vegas to come.

Soon after, the Cold War justified constructing the Nevada Test Site. Initially unconcerned about radiation fallout, Las Vegans took the atomic age in stride. Monthly above-ground atomic blasts shattered casino windows downtown and mushroom clouds rose on the horizon, while the newly minted 'Atomic City' crowned a 'Miss Atomic Bomb' beauty queen, sold 'atomburgers' and billed Elvis as the 'Atomic-Powered Singer.'

GANGSTERS & THE GOOD OL' DAYS

Get nostalgic for when mobsters and FBI G-men squared off in Vegas casinos' back alleys at downtown's brand-new **Mob Museum** (www.mobmuseum.org), set to open in 2011. The $50-million museum will inhabit the historic federal courthouse at 300 Stewart Ave, where the Kefauver Committee hearings, part of a federal investigation into organized crime, were held in 1951.

Interactive museum exhibits will investigate both sides of the city's underworld story. Uncover the truth about infamous Vegas mobsters like Meyer Lansky and Frank 'Lefty' Rosenthal, then learn about the law enforcement officials who chased 'em down (or else took part in the 'skim'). It's sure to be a hit, doll.

FROM MOBSTERS TO MEGARESORTS

Big-name entertainers like Frank Sinatra, Liberace and Sammy Davis Jr arrived on stage at the same time as topless French showgirls, while mob-backed tycoons upped the casino-glitz ante. In the face of mounting bad publicity from notorious links to organized crime, the gambling industry was given a much-needed patina of legitimacy when eccentric billionaire Howard Hughes made the high-profile purchase of the Desert Inn in 1967.

Spearheaded by Hughes' spending spree, corporate ownership of casinos blossomed and publicly traded companies bankrolled a building bonanza in the late 1960s and early '70s. The 1973 debut of the MGM Grand, later rebuilt as one of the world's largest hotels, and Steve Wynn's fabulous Mirage casino hotel opening in 1989 signaled that the age of the corporate 'megaresort' had dawned.

A MODERN MECCA

The 1990s saw the building boom on the Strip get even bigger, as the Luxor's gigantic black pyramid arose from the desert, the Stratosphere Tower became the tallest building in the western US, Paris Las Vegas erected its ersatz Eiffel Tower and the fountains of Bellagio started dancing.

The 21st century started off with an even bigger bang, as Steve Wynn imploded the vintage Desert Inn to make way for his eponymous mega-resort. In 2009 CityCenter transformed the Strip's skyline architecture with its new-modernist high-rises. Despite being bruised by the recent US recession, Las Vegas today boasts all but a few of the world's 20 biggest hotels and nearly 37 million visitors every year.

HERE TODAY, GONE TOMORROW

Structures that predate 1960 cling to Las Vegas like a trailer park hanging on for dear life during a tornado. Historic buildings are regularly blown to pieces with dynamite or slammed apart by wrecking balls, all to make way for new casino hotels and megaresorts.

Much like mushroom-cloud-viewing parties during Nevada's atomic age, modern-day implosions are an excuse to party on the Strip. Out with a bang, not a whimper, is the motto. Tourists can buy videos of famous implosions from years past and learn all about the tricky technical matters requiring hundreds of pounds of explosives.

Everyone is eager to know what's next on the chopping block. There's even a website devoted entirely to Las Vegas casino 'death watches': www.lvrevealed.com/deathwatch.

LIFE IN LAS VEGAS

Known as America's dirty little secret, Sin City is a bastion of naughty, hangover-inducing weekends for people from all walks of life. Nevada's biggest metropolis sells itself to tourists with the trademarked slogan 'What happens in Vegas, stays in Vegas.' Infamous for its historic mob ties, Sin City's bad reputation obscures its day-to-day realities.

All of that belies what is, at heart, a conservative cow town. Despite all images to the contrary, prostitution is illegal in Clark County. Gay and lesbian life is often hidden, remaining underground to avoid the wrath of the religious right. Racism has a long history in Las Vegas, too; it wasn't until the 1960s that the color line was crossed at the Strip's casino hotels.

Las Vegas is a youthful city. Most locals were born outside the state. Many are twenty- and thirtysomethings who only moved here within the last decade (including a surprising number from Hawaii). Due to the recent US economic downturn, accompanied by widespread unemployment and bank foreclosures on heavily mortgaged homes, Las Vegas now loses more residents each month than it gains. With so many new faces coming and going all the time, a disturbingly transient feeling permeates the city.

Lady Luck does not smile on everyone here. Las Vegas has been ranked as the 'meanest city in America' in which to be homeless. If you wander east of Fremont St or into the so-called 'Naked City' between downtown and the Strip, it won't take five minutes before you'll run into someone desperately in need of help: a crack-addicted prostitute looking to score, a babbling person pushing a shopping cart full of garbage bags or a de-generate gambler who's drunk off a 40oz beer can stuffed in a crumpled paper bag.

Nevada has the third-highest percentage of high-school dropouts in the country; since the local economy is fueled by minimum-wage workers, many teens think higher education won't help them get ahead. Fine arts and culture in Las Vegas would, until recently, have been just another oxymoron. That's no longer the case, however, with a thriving downtown arts scene, a couple of Smithsonian-affiliated museums and UNLV's Performing Arts Center.

Las Vegas is a city of die-hard sports fans, and there are scores of race and sports books inside casinos to prove it. The problem is, there aren't any professional home teams to root for. Most of the betting action is placed on national franchise teams, although UNLV college sports are big business. Everyone gets revved up for championship boxing matches on 'Fight Night.'

DOS & DON'TS

Polite requests will solve any problems you may have in Las Vegas faster than noisy complaints. For tipping practices, see the inside front cover.

The legal age for drinking and gambling is 21. You can buy booze everywhere 24/7.

No matter how old you are, always carry ID, especially for getting into bars and nightclubs. Open containers of alcohol are illegal in public but often overlooked, except in vehicles. Cops crack down on DUI (driving under the influence, whether of alcohol or drugs) with a vengeance; fines and sentences are stiff. On the street, more people are injured in crosswalks than in auto accidents.

Smoking cancer sticks is no longer permissible everywhere; stogie puffing is also restricted. Smoking is banned inside shopping malls, movie theaters, indoor areas of restaurants and bars serving food. If you don't see an ashtray, ask before lighting up. Hotels advertise nonsmoking guest rooms, but there are no guarantees – you may sniff more than a whiff of cigarettes inside 'em.

When movie stars first landed in Las Vegas in the 1950s, no lady would be caught dead in anything less than an evening gown once the cocktail hour arrived, and even off-duty showgirls dressed like starlets. Meanwhile, Sy Devore tailored European-style suits for the Rat Pack and even the janitors wore tuxedos at the Flamingo casino hotel. Today, dress codes exist only at high-end restaurants, trendy nightclubs and ultra lounges. T-shirts and jeans are the everyday norm for tourists.

GIRLS! GIRLS! GIRLS!

Prostitution was banned from Las Vegas in the 1940s, when the US military forced the closure of the city's brothels. But outgoing Mayor Oscar Goodman has gone on record with his pro-prostitution stance, saying that legalizing prostitution here would 'turn old motels into beautiful brothels.'

And then there's George Flint, an ordained minister who is Nevada's only paid lobbyist for the state's legal bordellos. His job is to see that attempts to end legal prostitution in Nevada, where it's still permitted in many rural counties, don't get too far.

Far from romantic Old West bordellos, most modern brothels are just double-wide trailers behind a barbed-wire fence at the side of a lonesome highway. For a real-life peek behind the scenes, read Alexa Albert's conflicted and disturbing *Brothel: Mustang Ranch and Its Women*, or watch HBO's bizarre reality-TV series *Cathouse*, now on DVD.

GOVERNMENT & POLITICS

In 1999, in a major blow to official public-relations efforts to clean up Sin City's image, Las Vegas voters elected long-time criminal defense lawyer Oscar Goodman to be their mayor. Goodman, who gained fame as a notorious legal shark defending mobster 'goodfellas' like Tony 'The Ant' Spilotro and Meyer Lansky, even portrayed himself in the movie *Casino*. What's less well-known is that Goodman also devoted much of his practice to the poor and the dispossessed, sometimes working pro bono.

The alleged 'barrister to butchers,' as an editorial in the *Las Vegas Review-Journal* described him, makes no effort to hide his past. Indeed, Mayor Goodman loves to talk about the old days. But he caught the voters' fancy with a populist platform calling for developers to pay fees to help solve the city's traffic and pollution woes. The mayor has also been a tireless proponent of the need to redevelop the downtown urban core.

After being re-elected to a third mayoral term with a landslide 83.69% of the vote in 2007, Goodman is still enjoying enormous popularity. He frequently uses the mayoral pulpit for fiery comments on hot-button political issues, such as legalizing prostitution. His more notorious achievements include getting his mug on a limited-edition casino chip, becoming a guest celebrity photographer for *Playboy* and hosting 'Martini with the Mayor' nights. Goodman will be a tough act to follow in 2011.

ENVIRONMENT

Las Vegas is an environmentalist's nightmare, the antithesis of a naturalist's vision of the US. Ironically, it's also the gateway to some of the Southwest's most spectacular natural attractions, such as the Grand Canyon.

Water usage is the chief concern. The city of Las Vegas receives the vast majority of its water from the Colorado River, which feeds Lake Mead. Some scientists have projected that the Las Vegas Valley has a 50/50 chance of exhausting its entire water supply by 2021.

Air pollution is an equally vexing topic: the valley is fringed by mountains that trap hazardous particles, and the city is often in violation of federal air-quality standards. On many days the sky harbors a dirty inversion layer, sometimes so thick that the mountains are barely visible. With traffic on the freeways and at McCarran International Airport on the rise, it's looking a lot like LA.

For more on 'greening' Las Vegas, see p173.

FURTHER READING

Few famous authors have hit the jackpot in Vegas, but gonzo journalist Hunter S Thompson (*Fear and Loathing in Las Vegas: A Savage Journey to the Heart of the American Dream*), 1960s countercultural narrator Tom Wolfe (*The Kandy-Kolored Tangerine-Flake Streamline Baby*), and pop novelist and screenwriter Mario Puzo (*The Godfather, Inside Las Vegas*) have all confronted the underbelly of the shimmering beast.

Scores of pulpy biographies have been written about the gangsters, movie stars and entertainers who pushed this dusty Nevada town into the spotlight, from gangster Bugsy Siegel to Elvis and beyond. *Rat Pack Confidential: Frank, Dean, Sammy, Peter, Joey and the Last Great Show Biz Party* by Shawn Levy has a swingin' style that echoes the hip stylings of the era. *Cult Vegas: The Weirdest! The Wildest! The Swingin'est Town on Earth* by Mike Weatherford, an entertainment reporter for the *Las Vegas Review-Journal*, revels in all of the offbeat trivia and celebrity gossip from the 1960s 'golden age.' *When the Mob Ran Vegas: Stories of Murder, Mayhem and Money* dishes fantastic dirt on Sin City's gangster era, all told by Mafia aficionado Steve Fischer.

Nicholas Pileggi's *Casino: Love and Honor in Las Vegas* tracks the true-crime story of the Chicago Mafia's move to take over Vegas, with all the bribery, book-making and mistresses leading in a downward spiral to disaster.

Equally dark in its outlook, John O'Brien's *Leaving Las Vegas* is a merciless novel about a desperate alcoholic and an equally damaged 'working girl.' In *Skin City: Behind the Scenes of the Las Vegas Sex Industry*, long-time resident Jack Sheehan interviews madams, strippers and XXX-film stars for what a reviewer called an 'erotic travelogue.'

> **VINTAGE VEGAS SOUNDTRACK**
> > 'Luck Be a Lady,' as recorded by Frank Sinatra
> > 'Viva Las Vegas,' as recorded by Elvis Presley
> > 'Ace in the Hole,' as recorded by Bobby Darin
> > 'The Lady is a Tramp,' as recorded by Sammy Davis Jr
> > 'I've Got You Under My Skin,' as recorded by Keely Smith and Louis Prima
>
> …or just about anything from Capitol Records' *The Rat Pack: Live at the Sands* album or the *Live from Las Vegas* series. For a red-light burlesque groove, the rare *Las Vegas Grind* series from Crypt Records (www.cryptrecords.com) should satisfy all of your naughty urges.

Titled as an homage to Upton Sinclair's muckraking novel *The Jungle*, Ed Reid and Ovid Demaris' *Green Felt Jungle* was an early indictment of casino corruption and lawless violence in Las Vegas during the 1940s, '50s and early '60s. Think all of the mobsters have left town and Vegas has been Disneyfied? *The Money and the Power: The Making of Las Vegas and Its Hold on America* by Sally Denton and Roger Morris is a haunting investigation of the city's underworld in the late 20th century.

For high-culture vultures, the landmark 1995 anthology *Literary Las Vegas*, edited by Mike Tronnes, features essays and short stories spanning 40 years, from atomic-bomb-viewing picnics to the wedding-chapel industry. Robert Venturi's classic *Learning from Las Vegas* was the first to celebrate the city's architecture as pop art, and *Viva Las Vegas: After-Hours Architecture* by Alan Hess is an illustrated history of pre-Luxor properties.

FILMS & TELEVISION

Less than 300 miles from Los Angeles, Las Vegas has long been a favorite shooting location for Hollywood. Maybe it's the sheer cinematic quality of the Strip, which resembles a giant movie set, that draws so many directors here.

Casino interiors were cast often by the industry in the 1940s, when Frank Sinatra made his silver-screen debut and movie mogul Howard Hughes frequently worked on location. Atomic testing captured the imagination of B-grade sci-fi directors in the 1950s. Sinatra's Rat Pack enjoyed frequent cameos, especially after their hijinks in the classic *Ocean's 11* (1960), and Elvis shook his thang in *Viva Las Vegas* (1964). James Bond glorified glitzy Vegas in *Diamonds are Forever* (1971), while the epic

Godfather (1972), written by self-described 'degenerate gambler' Mario Puzo, was the first flick to portray the Mafia in Las Vegas. Martin Scorsese delved deeper into mobster wars with *Casino* (1995).

In *Rain Man* (1988), Dustin Hoffman and Tom Cruise conspire to beat the house edge. In *Bugsy* (1991), Warren Beatty and Annette Bening bring to life the original Flamingo casino hotel. Obviously infatuated with Sin City, Nicolas Cage starred with Sarah Jessica Parker in *Honeymoon in Vegas* (1992) and Elizabeth Shue in the brutal *Leaving Las Vegas* (1995). The epitome of bad taste, Chevy Chase's *Vegas Vacation* (1997) nevertheless had a few redeeming cameos, including Wayne Newton and Siegfried and Roy on stage at the Mirage.

No movie rebirthed the contemporary cool of Vegas as much as *Swingers* (1996) did. The cinematic adaptation of Hunter S Thompson's classic *Fear and Loathing in Las Vegas* (1998), starring Johnny Depp and Benicio Del Toro, confirmed that sin was 'in' again. In a remake of the Sinatra classic *Ocean's Eleven* (2001), a star-studded cast including Brad Pitt, George Clooney and Julia Roberts plots to bilk a string of casinos. The independent flick *The Cooler* (2003), featuring William H Macy as a no-luck gambler and Alec Baldwin as a monstrous casino mogul, is all aces. Starring Kevin Spacey, *21* (2008) was inspired by the true story of card-counting college students who swindled Vegas casinos. *The Hangover* (2009) is a zany, bachelor-party-weekend comedy with an appearance by Mike Tyson.

The prime-time TV show *CSI: Crime Scene Investigation* sets fictionalized police forensic investigations against the backdrop of Vegas' neon lights. Reality TV has hit the city like an epidemic, most recently with pop illusionist Criss Angel's *Mindfreak*.

DIRECTORY
TRANSPORTATION
ARRIVAL & DEPARTURE
AIR

Las Vegas is served by **McCarran International Airport** (LAS; ☎ 261-5211; www.mccarran.com; 5757 Wayne Newton Blvd), just a crapshoot from the south end of the Strip, and a few smaller general aviation facilities around the city. McCarran ranks among the USA's 10 busiest airports. Most domestic airlines use Terminal 1; international, charter and some domestic flights depart from Terminal 2. Free trams link outlying gates. There are ATMs, a full-service bank, a post office, first-aid and police stations, the gym **Fitness Beast** (day pass $10; ⏰ 5am-11pm Mon-Fri, 8am-8pm Sat & Sun), free wi-fi internet access and slot machines with reputedly bad odds. Self-serve left-luggage lockers cost from $2 per hour up to $12 per day (48-hour maximum).

Taxi & Limousine

Taxis to Strip hotels (allow at least 30 minutes in heavy traffic) cost $15 to $20 (cash only, plus tip); fares to downtown run $20 to $25. The queue at the airport can be excruciatingly long; arriving passengers can usually find a skycap (airport porter) in the baggage-claim area, tip $5 or $10 per cart, then skip to the front of the line. 'Long-hauling' through the airport connector tunnel to I-15 is common; tell your taxi driver to use Paradise Rd or other direct surface routes. From the airport, it costs at least $45 per hour for a chartered sedan, or $55 for a six-person stretch limo, plus tip.

CLIMATE CHANGE & TRAVELING TO LAS VEGAS

Travel – especially air travel – is a significant contributor to global climate change. At Lonely Planet, we believe that all travelers have a responsibility to limit their personal impact. As a result, we have teamed with Rough Guides and other concerned industry partners to support Climate Care, which allows travelers to offset the greenhouse gases they are responsible for with contributions to energy-saving projects and other climate-friendly initiatives in the developing world. Lonely Planet offsets all staff and author travel.

At press time, flying or driving were almost the only ways to reach Sin City. **Greyhound** (☎ 800-231-2222; www.greyhound.com) offers inexpensive, but slow bus services from around the USA, arriving at a skeezy downtown **terminal** (☎ 384-9568; 200 S Main St). High-speed rail links between Southern California and Las Vegas along the heavily trafficked I-15 corridor have been proposed, but no dice yet.

For more information about responsible travel, visit www.lonelyplanet.com. For details on offsetting your carbon emissions and a carbon calculator, go to www.climatecare.org.

Bus

Notoriously slow airport-shuttle buses charge from $6.50 per person one way to the Strip or $8 to downtown hotels. Some airport shuttles operate 24 hours.

If you're traveling light, CAT's bus 108 runs 24/7 from the airport to the convention center, and Hilton and Sahara monorail stations ($2, 25 to 35 minutes), then continues downtown. Bus 109 runs 24/7 from the airport to the South Strip Transfer Terminal ($2, 10 minutes), where Ace Gold and Deuce buses depart for the Strip ($3).

LAND

By car it's about a 4½-hour drive (270 miles) from Los Angeles, five hours (330 miles) from San Diego and 9½ hours (570 miles) from San Francisco. Expect serious delays on weekends and holidays. For recorded road-condition updates, dial ☎ 877-687-6237 for Nevada and ☎ 800-427-7623 for California. Along the I-15 corridor through the Mojave Desert, Highway Radio (Barstow 98.1FM, Baker 99.5FM) broadcasts traffic and weather updates every half hour.

TRAVEL DOCUMENTS

Foreign visitors must have a machine-readable passport (usually with biometric identifiers) that is valid for at least six months beyond their planned exit date.

VISA

Visas aren't required for citizens of the 36 Visa Waiver Program countries (including Australia, Ireland, New Zealand, the UK and many other European nations), who may enter the USA for up to 90 days visa-free. However, citizens of these countries must still apply for travel authorization online (see https://esta.cbp.dhs.gov) at least 72 hours before their visit; this registration is valid for two years. Temporary visitors from Canada do not normally need a visa, but must bring their passport. All other foreign citizens must wrangle a nonimmigrant visa in advance from a US embassy or consulate. Double-check the mercurial requirements at http://travel.state.gov/visa.

RETURN/ONWARD TICKET

Travelers under the reciprocal Visa Waiver Program need round-trip or onward tickets to enter the US. Travelers applying for visas overseas will generally require such tickets as proof of their intent to skedaddle home.

GETTING AROUND

Las Vegas traffic is often gridlocked and the most heavily touristed areas are flat, so the best way to get around is on foot, in combination with occasional taxi, monorail or bus rides. In this book, the nearest monorail station (**M**) or bus route (**🚌**) is noted after the relevant icon with each listing.

BUS
Regional Transportation Commission of Southern Nevada (RTC; ☎ 228-7433, 800-228-3911; www.rtcsouthernnevada. com) buses operate from 5am to 2am daily, with popular Strip and downtown routes running 24/7. The fare is $2 ($3 for Ace or Deuce buses). Exact change is required (prepay before boarding Ace buses). Free maps and timetables are available from drivers and the **Downtown Transportation Center** (300 N Casino Center Blvd).

Some off-Strip casino hotels offer limited free shuttle buses to/from the Strip.

CAR
Heavy traffic makes navigating the city by car a chore, particularly during weekday rush hours and on weekends along the Strip. When traffic is snarled on I-15 and Las Vegas Blvd, stick to alternate surface routes. Listen to KNUU 'K-News' (970AM) for frequent traffic and weather updates. Free valet (tip at least $3) and/or self-parking are available almost everywhere in Las Vegas. If you've been drinking, **Designated Drivers** (☎ 702-456-7433; http://vegas.designated driversinc.com; ☉ 24hr) will pick you up and drive your car back to your hotel from $55, depending on mileage.

At press time, gas cost less than $3 per US gallon in Las Vegas. Economy car-rental rates start at around $25 per day or $135 per week, plus about $20 per day for insurance (usually optional). Corvettes and exotic convertibles fetch over $225 per day. Quoted rental rates may not include sales tax (8.1%), airport (10%) and government (12%) surcharges, or facility and vehicle fees ($4.40 per day). For weekends, reserve at least two weeks in advance.

Car-rental agencies with airport desks include **Alamo** (☎ 877-222-9075; www.alamo.com), **Budget** (☎ 800-922-2899; www.budgetvegas.com), **Dollar** (☎ 800-800-3665; www.dollar.com) and **Thrifty** (☎ 800-847-4389; www.thrifty.com). Airport pick-ups are usually cheaper than having a rental car delivered to your hotel. For something glamorous, ring **Las Vegas Exotic Car Rentals** (☎ 866-871-1893; www.exoticcarrentalslasvegas.com; 10177 W Charleston Blvd).

MONORAIL & TRAM
A private **monorail** (☎ 699-8299; www .lvmonorail.com; ☉ 7am-2am Mon-Thu, 7am-3am Fri-Sun) links some Strip casino resorts, speedily shuttling between the MGM Grand, Bally's/Paris, the Flamingo, Harrah's/Imperial Palace, the city's convention center, the Hilton and the Sahara. One-way rides cost $5.

Free air-conditioned trams shuttle between the Bellagio, CityCenter and Monte Carlo; TI (Treasure Island) and the Mirage; and Excalibur, Luxor and Mandalay Bay.

TAXI

It's illegal to hail a cab on the street. Taxi stands are found at casino, hotel and shopping-mall entrances. Fares (cash only) are metered: flagfall is $3.30 plus $2.40 per mile and 50¢ per minute while waiting. A lift from one end of the Strip to the other, or from mid-Strip to downtown, runs from $12 to $16, plus tip. Reputable companies include **Yellow Cab** (☎ 873-2000). File any complaints via http://taxi.state.nv.us.

TRAVEL PASSES

One-/three-day monorail passes cost $12/28. RTC's all-access 24-/72-hour bus pass is $7/15.

PRACTICALITIES
BUSINESS HOURS

Open 24/7/365 is the rule at casino hotels. Normal business hours are 9am to 5pm on weekdays. Some banks and post offices stay open later and on Saturday mornings. Retail shopping hours are 10am to 9pm (to 6pm Sunday); casino shops stay open until 11pm or

later. Christmas is one of the few holidays on which most non-casino businesses close.

DISCOUNTS

The biggest discounts are 'comps' handed out by casinos to members of players' clubs and 'rated' gamblers. Casino 'fun books' given to hotel guests are a grab bag of small coupons. Hotel rooms provide complimentary copies of tourist mags that are a source of bigger discounts (eg half-price or two-for-one admission) on shows, restaurants and attractions. Some casino resorts offer special discounts via Twitter, Facebook pages and mobile-phone text messages, if you sign up.

A **Las Vegas Power Pass** (☎ 800-490-9330; www.visiticket.com; adult/child from $78/45) may be worthwhile if you plan to visit a *lot* of big-ticket attractions and museums; it even lets you skip the lines at some of them. Don't bother buying the MealTicket, though.

ELECTRICITY

Electrical current in the USA is 110V AC (60Hz). North American electrical goods have plugs with two (flat) or three (two flat, one round) pins. Consult www.kropla .com for information about converters and adapters.

EMERGENCIES

On the Strip and the Fremont Street Experience, police and private security officers are out in force, and surveillance cameras (the 'eye in the sky') are omnipresent. Utilize in-room hotel safes and never leave valuables unattended, especially while gambling. Beware of pickpockets in crowds (eg on public transportation). If you wander away from Fremont St downtown, keep your wits about you, day and night.

For emergencies:

Police, fire, ambulance (☎ 911)
Police (non-emergency) (☎ 311)
Rape Crisis Center (☎ 366-1640)

For minor ailments and injuries, it's less expensive to go to a walk-in clinic than a hospital emergency room. East of the Strip, **Harmon Medical Center** (☎ 796-1116; 150 E Harmon Ave; ◷ 8am-5pm Mon-Fri) offers limited translation services. Emergency contraception services are available without a prescription from **Planned Parenthood** (☎ 547-9888; Suite 25, 3300 E Flamingo Rd).

HOLIDAYS

New Year's Day January 1
Martin Luther King Jr Day Third Monday in January
Presidents' Day Third Monday in February
Easter Sunday March/April
Memorial Day Last Monday in May
Independence Day July 4
Labor Day First Monday in September
Columbus Day Second Monday in October
Veterans' Day November 11
Thanksgiving Day Fourth Thursday in November
Christmas Day December 25

INTERNET

Most hotel business centers charge an arm and a leg for 24/7 internet access. High-speed wired/wireless internet access in hotel rooms typically costs $12 to $15 per 24 hours. You'll find free wi-fi at only a few casino hotels, such as the Venetian and Palazzo. Cheap internet cafes hide inside Strip souvenir shops south of Harmon Ave, and across from the UNLV campus along Maryland Parkway. Otherwise, try **FedEx Office** (☎ 951-2400; 395 Hughes Center Dr; per min 20-30¢; ◷ 24hr), which also has branches downtown and at the city's convention center.

For the lowdown on what's happening on the Strip and around town, check out casino hotels' Facebook pages and Twitter feeds, online versions of local newspapers and magazines (see p193), and popular websites, including the following:

Cheapo Vegas (www.cheapovegas.com)
Las Vegas Advisor (www.lasvegasadvisor.com)
LVCVA (www.visitlasvegas.com)
Vegas Deluxe (www.vegasdeluxe.com)
VegasChatter (www.vegaschatter.com)
Vegas.com (www.vegas.com)

MONEY

Casinos exist to separate you from your dough and will facilitate that end any way they can. Transaction fees at ATMs inside gaming areas are high ($3.50 or more). All casinos will advance cash against plastic, but fees are exorbitant – don't do it. To avoid surcharges, use your debit card to get cash back when making purchases at noncasino businesses like convenience stores and pharmacies.

For currency exchange rates, see the inside front cover of this book. Casino-hotel fees to exchange foreign currency are higher than at banks but lower than at most exchange bureaus. **American Express** (☎ 739-8474; Fashion Show, 3200 Las Vegas Blvd S; ☘ 10am-9pm Mon-Fri, 10am-8pm Sat, 11am-6pm Sun) has competitive rates.

The average visitor's daily budget is $230. Accommodations may be your biggest expense, and hotel room rates go up and down like the stock market (see p164). Meals cost at least $10, though top-end restaurants easily run over $100 per person. You don't need to rent a car, except for jaunts outside the city (see p155). For more tips on saving money at attractions and on dining and entertainment, see p191.

NEWSPAPERS & MAGAZINES

Nevada's largest daily newspaper is the conservative *Las Vegas Review-Journal* (www.lvrj.com), which publishes with the tabloid *Las Vegas Sun* (www.lasvegassun.com); look for the former's Friday 'Neon' entertainment guide. Free tabloids *Las Vegas Weekly* (www.lasvegasweekly.com) and weekly *Las Vegas CityLife* (www.lasvegascitylife.com) cover local news, nightlife, music, film, the arts and more. Free monthly magazine *944* (www.944.com/lasvegas) tracks celebs, clubs and hot spots, while weekly *Vegas Seven* (http://weeklyseven.com) covers arts and culture, eating and entertainment. *Vegas* (www.vegasmagazine.com) targets fashionistas, casino moguls and celebrities.

ORGANIZED TOURS

Gray Line (☎ 384-1234, 800-634-6579; www.graylinelasvegas.com) Runs the popular 'Neon Lights' night-time city bus tour, which lasts six hours ($55); stops include the Bellagio's fountains and downtown's Fremont Street Experience.

Haunted Vegas Tours (☎ 339-8744, reservations 866-218-4935; www.hauntedvegastours.com; 2½hr show & tour $66; ☘ 9:30pm daily) Most folks are disappointed by the campy sideshow, but the after-dark bus trip around Sin City visits the haunts of Liberace and gangster Bugsy Siegel.

Jubilee! Backstage Tour (☎ 800-237-7469; Bally's, 3645 Las Vegas Blvd S; 1hr tour $15; ☘ 11am Mon, Wed & Sat) Escorted by a real-life stage performer, Bally's takes you behind the scenes of Vegas' long-running $50-million showgirl revue, *Jubilee!*

Papillon Grand Canyon Helicopters
(☎ 736-7243, 888-635-7272; www.papillon
.com) Offers 10-minute jetcopter flyovers of
the Strip (from $99).

Vegas Mob Tour (☎ 339-8744, reservations
866-218-4935; www.vegasmobtour.com;
2½hr film & tour $57; ☽ 6pm daily) This
night-time city bus tour revels in the sordid
history of when the Mafia really ran this town.

TELEPHONE

The only mobile (cellular) phones
that will work in Las Vegas are
tri-/quad-band models operating on local US-specific GSM and
CDMA frequencies, which vary.
Most North American visitors can
use their cell phones in Las Vegas,
but check with your carrier about
roaming charges before you start
racking up minutes. Using cell
phones near casino race and sports
books is prohibited by law. On the
Strip, some hotel business centers
rent out cell phones to guests.

Public phones are mostly
coin-operated; some accept credit
cards or have dataports for laptop
and PDA internet access. Local
calls generally cost 50¢. If calling a
long-distance number outside the
local area code (☎ 702), dial ☎ 1
first. Pharmacies and convenience
stores sell prepaid phonecards,
but they can be rip-offs – check
the fine print for hidden fees and
surcharges. Major carriers like **AT&T**
(☎ 800-321-0288) can facilitate long-
distance calls.

COUNTRY & CITY CODES
City code (☎ 702)
Country code (☎ 1)

USEFUL PHONE NUMBERS
Local Operator (☎ 0)
International Operator (☎ 00)
International Direct Dial Code (☎ 011)
Local Directory Assistance (☎ 411)
Long-distance Directory Assistance
(☎ 1 + area code + 555-1212)
Toll-free Directory Assistance
(☎ 800-555-1212)

TIPPING
Service-industry staff rely on
tips to bring their incomes up
to decent levels, while fortunes
have been made by valet-parking
concession owners. You should
only withhold tips in cases of outrageously poor service, however.
See the inside front cover of this
guidebook for advice on who to
tip, and how much.

TOURIST INFORMATION
Many tour operators push unof-
ficial 'visitor information,' but
there's only one official city tourism
agency: **Las Vegas Convention & Visitors
Authority** (LVCVA; ☎ 892-0711, 877-847-
4858; www.visitlasvegas.com; 3150 Paradise
Rd; ☽ office 8am-5pm, toll-free hotline
7am-7pm). The hotline provides up-
to-date information about shows,
attractions, activities and more, and
staff may be able to help with finding last-minute accommodations.

TRAVELERS WITH DISABILITIES

Vegas has the most ADA-accessible guestrooms in the USA. Unless otherwise noted, all attractions listed in this book are wheelchair-accessible. Wheelchair seating is widely available and assisted listening devices are offered at most showrooms. Most public transportation and several hotel pools are lift-equipped. By law, all taxi companies must have a wheelchair-accessible van. If you're driving, bring your disabled-parking placard from home. Guide dogs may be brought into restaurants, hotels and businesses. Some payphones are equipped for the hearing-impaired. For more info, contact the LVCVA's ADA coordinator at ☎ 892-0711 (☎ TTY 486-1018, ☎ voice relay 800-326-6888).

>INDEX

See also separate subindexes for Casinos (p200), See (p201), Shop (p201), Eat (p202) and Play (p203).

000 map pages

rides 81-4, *see also* See *subindex*
Rio 58
Riviera 68
roulette 38

S
Sahara 59
salons 147-9, *see also* Play *subindex*
Sam's Town 68-9
shopping 87-99, *see also* Shop *subindex*
shows, *see* Play *subindex*
Siegel, Benjamin 'Bugsy' 46, 180
Silverton 69
slot machines 39
souvenirs 16, 167
spas 147-9, *see also* Play *subindex*
spectacles, *see* See *subindex*
sports 149-50, 151, *see also* Play *subindex*
sports books 37, 39
Spring Mountain Ranch State Park 160
Springs Preserve 24-5, 76
steakhouses, *see* Eat *subindex*
Stratosphere 60, 115
Stratosphere Tower 23, 84
Strip, the 9, 12-13, **206-7**
strip clubs 150, 152, *see also* Play *subindex*

T
taxis 191
telephone services 194

Texas Hold'em 175
thrill rides, *see* See *subindex*
TI (Treasure Island) 61, 115
ticket-booking agencies 131
tipping 194, *see also* inside front cover
tourist information 194
tours 146, 161, 193-4
trams 190-1
transportation 188-91
travel passes 191
Tropicana 69
TV 186-7

U
ultra lounges 152-4, *see also* Play *subindex*

V
vacations 192
Valley of Fire 158
Vegas Club 69
Venetian 62, 116-17
video poker 39
visas 189

W
websites 179, 192
weddings 84-5, 168-9, *see also* See *subindex*
wildlife 77-8, *see also* See *subindex*
World Series of Poker 58, 133, 175
Wynn & Encore 63, 117-18

CASINOS
Bally's 64
Bellagio 42, 102-3
Bill's Gamblin' Hall & Saloon 64

Binion's 64
Caesars Palace 43, 103-4
California 65
Casino Royale 65
Circus Circus 44
El Cortez 65
Excalibur 45
Flamingo 46
Golden Gate 65-6
Golden Nugget 47
Hard Rock 48
Harrah's 66
Imperial Palace 66
Luxor 49, 107
Main Street Station 67
Mandalay Bay 50, 107-8
MGM Grand 51, 108-9
Mirage 52, 109-10
Monte Carlo 67
New York–New York 53, 110
Orleans 67
Palazzo 54, 111-13
Palms 55
Paris Las Vegas 56, 113-14
Planet Hollywood 57, 114
Plaza 67-8
Red Rock Casino Resort Spa 68
Rio 58
Riviera 68
Sahara 59
Sam's Town 68-9
Silverton 69
Stratosphere 60, 115
TI (Treasure Island) 61, 115
Tropicana 69
Vegas Club 69
Venetian 62, 116-17
Wynn & Encore 63, 117-18

000 map pages

⊙ SEE

000 map pages

000 map pages

>MAPS

Revel in the nonstop carnival atmosphere of Las Vegas